Frank Chapman Bliss

Queen Esther

And Other Poems

Frank Chapman Bliss

Queen Esther
And Other Poems

ISBN/EAN: 9783744705417

Printed in Europe, USA, Canada, Australia, Japan

Cover: Foto ©Thomas Meinert / pixelio.de

More available books at **www.hansebooks.com**

QUEEN ESTHER,

AND

OTHER POEMS.

BY

FRANK C. BLISS.

TO

MY DAUGHTER,

MRS. E. B. KENNEDY,

OF

BLOOMFIELD, N. J.,

THIS VOLUME IS AFFECTIONATELY

DEDICATED,

BY

THE AUTHOR.

CONTENTS.

	PAGE.
QUEEN ESTHER,	11
LESSONS OF LIFE,	105
IN MEMORIAM,	183
THE MISER'S FATE,	191
MIDNIGHT TRAGEDY,	194
WESTMINSTER,	197
GIVE US THIS DAY, OUR DAILY BREAD,	200
REFLECTIONS,	203
LIFE AND DEATH,	205
CHRISTMAS HYMN,	207

QUEEN ESTHER.

ACT I.

SCENE FIRST—IN THE PALACE SHUSHAN.

KING AHASUERUS. (*To himself.*)

Three years upon my throne
Have I now sat, conqueror, and ruler
Of mighty provinces. Vast my Empire!
From Caspian Sea to Indian Ocean,—
From India to Ethiopia
It now extends. In riches, how exhaustless
In arms, how powerful! for all the powers
Of Media and of Persia but do my

Bidding. 'Tis the Imperial Throne where sat
The noble Cyrus, who Asia conquered,
And with his fiery hosts pulled down the walls
And towers of proud and haughty Babylon.
In this my palace Shushan, the abode
Of former Kings, 'tis fit I should announce
The glory of my kingdom,—its riches
And its power. No longer will I rest
In proud, unsocial solitude, for Kings
And Monarchs, like the great orb of day, will
Shine in vain, if unseen—unhonored.
                    I love dominion,
Pride and power, and to my heart's content
I'll use them! Before me yet shall bow,
As subjects and as slaves, one hundred petty
Kings to learn their Master's will,—revolving
Round me, like stars about the sun.
Ho! my attendants.

(Enter Mehumen, Biztha, Harbona, Bigtha, and others—the King's Chamberlains—bowing.)

MEHUMEN.

What is our Sovereign's pleasure?

Queen Esther.

THE KING.

Make instant preparations
For a feast, sumptuous, princely, regal,
Worthy of Earth's Imperial Monarch—
One that will eclipse the dazzling, gorgeous
Banquet of my famous predecessor.
For our many guests, the gold and silver
Beds prepare, and bring ye forth the royal
Wines, with goblets, vases, and the thousand
Vessels of purest gold, now lying dust-
Covered in the secret closets. Burnish
To dazzling brightness, the golden sceptre,
And jeweled diadem; with fresh flowers,
With opening blossoms, with fragrant shrubbery
Bedeck our hanging gardens—scatter round
Arabia's sweet perfumes, her frankincense
And myrrh—in halls and niches, have arranged
Images of ivory, of ebony
And gold, from conquered Ethiopia brought.
In great abundance, gather the choicest
Viands—the rare luxuries of the East,
And for the space of one hundred, four score
Days let the feast continue. Yea, more! Send

Forth the heralds, and let rulers, nobles,
Princes, scattered throughout the provinces,
At the feast appear—homage pay to him
Whose word alone is law. *The King commands
Their presence.*

MEHUMEN.

It shall be done, O King!
As thou commandest.

THE KING.

Let there be no delay!
If not well done, thine head shall pay the forfeit.
But further I command; when have expired
These days of banqueting, another feast
Be given in the great garden-court, next
To our royal palace. Have it prepared;
Festooned about with hangings of crimson,
White, green and blue, made fast to silver rings
And marble pillars, by cords of purple
Linen, finest in texture. Let there be
Pavements reared, of red and blue, white and black
Marble, and place thereon cushions of gold

And silver, while in convenient corners,
On golden tripods, set up the massive,
Frosted basins—beside them precious ointments,
And ewers richly embossed, with perfumed
Waters filled. Our guests, dust-covered, traveling
From afar, will find them useful.
                                    Twine everywhere around,
Necklaces of choicest flowers, with wreaths
And garlands of divers forms, and colors
Variegated. Clusters of grapes, composed
Of jewels, pearls, and precious stones, bring from
Our Babylonian palace, and hang
Them o'er our golden throne—let fountains play,
Forth sending mist-like spray and sparkling streams,
Cooling and most refreshing. Ten thousand
Colored lights prepare, and thickly string them
Out 'mong branches of the trees, in hanging
Gardens, from palace windows, from every
Marble pillar, and let those brilliants shine
With dazzling brightness, making our palace
Shushan, like the great city of the Sun,
Beautiful and lovely. From highest mountain
Tops, all round about, let fires be kindled,

And to the GREAT SUPREME, who rules the spheres
And the celestial planets we adore,
Let sacrifice be offered.
   For seven long days and nights,
Shall last this garden banquet. Hasten now
And do my bidding, and at the proper
Time, to this great second feast, invite both
Great and small, for all shall come and homage
Pay to me, their Sovereign.

     MEHUMEN.

   We go, most gracious Sovereign!
To perform thy will and purposes.

      (Exeunt attendants.)

SCENE SECOND—ROOM IN MORDECAI'S DWELLING.

   MORDECAI. *(To himself.)*

      From my birth,
In mind—in spirit, I have worn the chains
Of slavery. A freedman, some may say
I am. 'Tis but an insult to our race,

For what is freedom without human rights?
Worse than a knavish beggar in the streets,
I'm laughed at, mocked, derided, scorned. The words,
"There goes the heathen Jew," in tones bitter
And sarcastic, strike deep within my soul
And make me sick at heart. But yesterday,
A tinseled knave dancing about the Court,
Dared utter words against our Jewish race,
Which drove the blood, hot, boiling through my veins,
And woke the Devil in me. I would have
Struck him dead, though rack and gibbet should have
Been my doom; but my good angel Esther,—
In thought, rose in my mind—my passions cooled
And kept me quiet. For my adopted
Daughter's sake, and to fulfill the solemn
Pledge I gave my dear kinsman, her father
On his death-bed—safely to guard, protect,
Instruct her—hard though it be—to treatment
Such as this, I must submit.
        How long, thou great Jehovah!
Must this heavy curse upon Thy chosen

People rest? 'Tis fourscore years since they were
By proud Nebuchadnezzar, sent captive
Into Babylon, who, in his fiendish
Hate, destroyed Jerusalem—in pieces
Breaking the golden vessels and burning
Solomon's Temple, to Thee, dedicated ;
    Most just and righteous are Thy judgments,
For we transgressed Thy law, and Judah's king
Jeconiah, did, as his fathers did,
Great evil in Thy sight, and Thou dids't send
Him captive with us. Mercies, Thou hast shown,
For which we bless Thee! Our tyrant Master,
In the plain of Dura, most impiously
A golden statue raised, commanding all
To bow and worship. Swift was Thy vengeance,
For forth he went a raving maniac—
With brutes he herded, till his hairs became
Like eagles' feathers, and his nails like claws
Of birds, and like an ox did he eat grass
Yea, more! the good and mighty Cyrus, Thou
Did'st raise, an instrument to do Thy will
Among the Nations of the Earth. Down he
Came on boasting Babylon, resistless

As the thunderbolt, and swift as lightning,
E'en while Belshazzar, the licentious king,
Was gazing with his midnight revelers
At words, "MENE, MENE, TEKEL, UPHARSIN,"
Written on the wall, by hand mysterious.
Belshazzar fell, and with him, this harlot
City. Then went there forth the just decree,
Freedom to captive Jews. Had Cyrus lived,
We should have been free indeed. Chains we wear
Not, but still are slaves, for like serpents' fangs,
This strong, cursed prejudice against our race
Is poisoning its very life-blood.
       Like aged oak
Rocked to and fro, by whirlwinds and by storms,
So must these feeble limbs a few years more
Withstand the scorn, and buffets of the world.
For myself I care not, but for Esther,
The fair and lovely maiden, whose many
Virtues, winning, modest ways and gentle
Manners, like cords have bound her to my heart,
I fear and tremble, for should her matchless
Charms and radiant loveliness, be, by some
Heathen dog discovered, like a pet lamb,

Innocent and guileless, she would be led
To slaughter; yea, be sacrificed upon
The altar of his passions.   But hark!
She comes!

(Enter Esther.)

ESTHER.

Thou here?   I thought thee absent,
Dearest of fathers!   Go not out to-day!
My heart with very joy doth throb, when thou
Art present with me.

MORDECAI.

I would be always with thee
If happiness it gave; but life hath cares
And stern necessities, which must not be
Ignored.   We must have food and raiment,
And like the busy ant and bee, daily
I labor to provide some future store.

ESTHER.

Have we not enough
For years to keep us in our simple style

Of living? To see thee toil and labor,
Embrowned by blazing sun, brow seamed with care,
And hands hardened in menial service, brings
Sorrow to my heart, and casts a shadow
O'er my soul. Could I but toil for thee, or had
I wealth to scatter along thy pathway,
How joyous my life ; for always with thee,
I could watch thy slow, and faltering steps
As wintry age came on, and for all wants
Provide.

MORDECAI.

I doubt thee not, fair
Daughter of a noble, but a misjudged
Race. Kings cannot boast of blood more royal,
Or more pure than that which courses through thy
Veins, thou soul of Innocence—of women
The most virtuous.

ESTHER.

Hast thou faith in dreams?

MORDECAI.

In nothing have I faith,
Save God and thee. But wherefore ask?

ESTHER.

Last night I had a dream;
So strange, so real did it seem, that when
I woke I could not drive it from my mind,
And still it haunts me. Methought I wandered
Forth, one bright and sunny day, to gather
Violets and pale lilies from the fields,
With which to deck our humble mansion.
Joyous and thoughtless as the singing birds
Around, onward I went o'er hill and vale,
Through verdant meadow and up grassy slopes,
Plucking the wild flowerets which seemed to smile
Sweetly upon me. The lengthening shadows,
And the sun far down the western slope, brought
Back my thoughts and bade me hasten to return.
Quickly I turned, my footsteps to retrace,
But all had changed. Hill, vale, the green verdure,
And music of the birds were gone. Alone
I stood, in a vast, wild and trackless desert,
'Mid arid sands, while from afar still blazed
The angry setting sun—seemed like the eye
Of God, throwing His burning glances thwart
A sinful world. Trembling, helpless, hopeless,

Like some shipwrecked wretch cast on a barren
Shore, I felt that I was lost. Oh! how my
Heart did throb and my pulse beat, as if some
Raging fever burned within, while the brain
Seemed bursting, from the hot blood that pressed it.
   Mine eyes I raised to heaven,
And there a speck I saw, like tiny cloud
Far distant in the air. Nearer to earth
It came, circles describing of a large
Extent. It was a monster bird, with wings
Wide spread, and of prodigious size and strength.
Now hovering o'er me, motionless it seemed,
For I could see its cold, black eye gazing
Serpent-like upon its prey, then circling
Round with a wild screech, like fiend incarnate,
Down it swooped upon me; then skyward went
The proud eagle, with its talons fastened
In my dress, bearing me far distant 'bove,
The clouds, to high and rugged cliffs where foot
Of man had never trod.
   Almost bereft of sense,
In a great warm nest, among the eaglets
I was laid, which cuddled with feathery

Softness round me, seemingly delighted.
And thus all night I lay, with my head out
From 'neath the wings of the great, powerful
Bird that brooded us, upward gazing at
The large convex of Chaldean sky, crowned
With twinkling stars, which brightly shone till dimmed
By the red streaks of morning light. Soon from
The east up rose the giant Sun, and with
His burning eye scanned the earth o'er till on
The rugged cliff it rested, and on us
The focus, like angry God, a stream he
Hurled, of hot, burning, scorching rays of light,
Like flame concentrated. We were consumed;
No! not consumed; but purified, transformed—
Perhaps evolutionized.
    All, methought had changed.
The eagle was a man, in kingly robes
With crown and sceptre, and his word was law,
While round his throne, as nobles and as lords,
Were the young eaglets to perform his will.
Your daughter Esther had become a queen,
And on the throne beside the King she sat—

His loving wife, and sharer of his joys
And sorrows. Even the nest, my prison
For one night, was like the Palace Shushan—
Most beautiful and lovely. Yea! I dreamed
That power and riches I possessed, which
Freely did I give to benefit our
Race ; and you my father, were to honor
Raised and greatly favored by the King.
This was my dream, painful, yet delightful.
What think you of it?

MORDECAI.

Dreams are but visions
Of the mind, which come and go like summer
Clouds—mere phantoms of the brain, most vivid
In conception, and varied in imagery.
God never sleeps! Nor does the soul immortal,
For while the passions rest, and senses sleep,
The mind is ever active, wandering
At will 'mong by-gone days, and scenes long since
Forgotten. It can no more rest, than can
The heart, which ever throbs, driving the life-
Blood through the system, or pulse, which ever

Beats, so long as health and life continue.
Most fearfully and wonderfully made
Is the human frame. Both in its system
Corporeal, and in its operations
It is complex, and little do we know
Respecting it. Forget thy dream, and blot
It from your mind.

ESTHER.

I cannot! It seems prophetic.

MORDECAI.

To me it seems like visions, spectres,
Seen only by some hypochondriac.
But Esther go not out unveiled ; thy charms
Might catch the eye of noble, or of prince,
Who gladly in thine ear would breathe the foul
Pollution of the Court ; besides, I hear
That in the palace a sumptuous feast
Is ordered, and the King his heralds sends
Into the provinces, commanding all
To come—prince, noble, ruler, and do him
Homage for one hundred and fourscore days.

ESTHER.

I never go unveiled!
Our ancient custom, do I most strictly
Follow.

MORDECAI.

Excuse me now; for a little while
Must I go forth—soon will return and seek
Thy loved companionship.
(*Exeunt.*)

SCENE THIRD—QUEEN'S APARTMENTS IN THE PALACE.

Vashti the Queen, and Sylvania her maid.

SYLVANIA. (*Entering.*)

There have arrived
The King's chamberlains, and outside await
Your royal will. Permission they do ask,
In person to present a message from
Our sovereign.

C

QUEEN VASHTI.

What message can they have,
And why so many sent, as if it were
A ponderous load? but hither bring my veil,
And cast it o'er me;—now bid them enter.
<small>(*Enter Mehumen, Biztha, Harbona, Bigtha and Abagtha—the King's chamberlains—bowing.*)</small>

VASHTI.

A message from the King?
What is my sovereign's pleasure?

MEHUMEN,

'Tis the seventh day
Of the great garden-feast, and his majesty—
Our sovereign, commands thy royal presence,
And has sent us, thee to accompany
With the crown royal. To lords and princes,
And to all the people, he would exhibit
Thy matchless beauty. This, his signet-ring
Shows our authority,

QUEEN VASHTI.

The ring I recognize;
But most strange it is, that he such message

Should have sent—commanding me, his Queen,
Unveiled, uncovered, to appear before
The motley crowd, now present at the feast.
Surely, it cannot be!

MEHUMEN.

Such was his command,
And with it gave this ring,—bade us hasten
Our departure, and with us bring the Queen.

QUEEN VASHTI.

What said the King?
Give me his message, word by word.

MEHUMEN.

He was seated
On his banquet throne, in the great palace
Garden. Gathered there upon his right and left
At feast reclining, were nobles, princes,
Rulers, who had come from distant provinces
With their attendants; and of the lower
Ranks, thousands were present. The King seemed
    flushed
With wine, and midst the revelry, to his

Presence called us. "Go to the Queen," said he,
"Give her this signet-ring, and bid her come
At once, and crown our banquet with her most
Gracious smile, and matchless beauty. Hasten!
And with the crown royal bring her. The King
Commands,—let her obey,"—those were his words.

QUEEN VASHTI.

I am a Queen!
And in my veins flows royal blood. As Queen,
Obedient have I ever been to him,
My lord and sovereign;—for nothing has he
Asked unjust, improper. But now, all flushed
With wine, the mistress of his throne he would
Degrade, and on her brow would stamp gross shame
And infamy; I will not stoop to acts
Base and ignoble in themselves, which blot
Out modesty, virtue cheapen, and which
The rules and customs of our land forbid.

MEHUMEN.

If I have grace of speech,
Which oft has served my country, and my King,—
And would serve you, most sacred majesty,

Oh! let me urge you to obey this stern,
But royal mandate,—unjust, ungracious
As it is.

QUEEN VASHTI.

    It is impossible!
Custom forbids that we attend these feasts,
Or before strangers stand unveiled. I am
No slave polluted, for the tinseled throng
To gaze at, nor before these licentious
Princes of the court will I now debase
My womanhood.

MEHUMEN.

    Without you, we tremble to return,
For the King's wrath is terrible.

QUEEN VASHTI.

    Have no fears for me, for sooner
Than obey this royal mandate, I will
Cast the Crown from off my head, and trample
It in the dust beneath my feet. Go! tell
The King, he wounds his honor, tarnishes
His throne, degrades his manhood, when he seeks

To make his Queen the gazing stock of those
Vile, drunken revelers.—You can depart.

(Exeunt chamberlains.)

(The Queen takes off her veil, and throws herself weeping upon a couch. Enters Sylvania.)

SYLVANIA.

My Royal Mistress weeping!
What mean these tears, now coursing down thy cheeks?—
Sure heralds of a sorrowing heart.

QUEEN VASHTI.

I am sick at heart!
Would that I were dead, and in the cold grave
Forgotten.

SYLVANIA.

Dead, and forgotten! Remember whom
Thou art, and who thy husband is, and then
Dry up your tears. You are not unequal
To the noblest task.

QUEEN VASHTI.

Think not Sylvania, that without cause
I weep, and seem so broken-hearted. Thou
Hast been ever dear to me, and art still

My loved companion, though thou dost perform
The menial service of a maid. When crowned
A Queen, unto myself I vowed in all
Things to obey my sovereign's will,—conscience
Permitting,—and well you know I have this
Vow performed. The King has been a loving,
Kind protector, and his commands have not
Been disobeyed. But alas! what fearful
Change; the sun-light of my heart is now puffed
Out by the dark storm-cloud, and my summer-
Days blasted, as if by winter's frosts.

SYLVANIA.

What means my mistress—
Thou art still Queen?

QUEEN VASHTI.

I am, but to-morrow
May not be. The King has pride, has power,
And an imperious will. These harden
Kings, insensibly to tyrants. Inflamed
By wine, he bade me to appear unveiled
Before him at the garden feast, and like
A gew-gaw, there to be exhibited.

SYLVANIA.

   What folly! and what an insult
To you my mistress!

  QUEEN VASHTI.

   These men,—his chamberlains, he sent
To bring the message, and be an escort
To me; I have refused to go—my blood
Shall stop, and stagnate in my heart before
I change my purpose. On my infant mind,
My mother's hand traced the faint characters
Of virtue and of modesty, which time
Has deepened into strength,—so deep, that death
Alone can blur them. But enough of this,—
Come with me into the ante-chamber.
        (*Exeunt.*)

ACT II.

Scene First—the garden of the palace.

(King, Lords, Nobles, and Princes at the feast.)

KING.

How fare my honored guests,
And faithful subjects? What can I do more
To give you pleasure, and your hearts to fill
With joy and gladness? Let the cup-bearers
Come, our goblets fill again with choicest
Wine,—the sparkling juice of Egypt's grapes.
'Tis our last night of banqueting, and we
Would have it pass in wildest merriment.
The Queen will soon be here, and the last toast
Shall be her health and happiness,—for ever
Hath she been my most obedient subject.

(Enter Mehumen, and other chamberlains.)

Where is the Queen? Without her, why return?

MEHUMEN.

      Most mighty Sovereign!
Upon our bended knees, pardon we crave
For our offence, if in thy sight offence
It should appear, because we bring her not.

KING.

      What! comes she not?
By my soul, 'tis very strange!—explain!

MEHUMEN.

      Obeying thy commands,
We called upon her majesty,—showed her
The signet-ring, and message gave, but she
Refused here to appear, unveiled before
The guests. We urged her strongly, but could not
Change her purpose. Custom, she said, forbade
Her to appear, as did her modesty,
And virtue.

KING.

     Such presumptuous virtue
My pride provokes, and what is custom when
My will opposes? Did she say no more?

Queen Esther.

MEHUMEN.

She blushed, and trembled, and grew pale,
But with a voice clear and determined, said,
" I will not stoop to acts, base and ignoble
In themselves, nor before the licentious
Princes of the court debase my womanhood.
Go! tell the King, that manhood he degrades,
Tarnishes his throne, and wounds his honor,
When he seeks to make his Queen the laughing-
Stock of midnight revelers."

KING.

God of my fathers!
Was it to me, her monarch, that she sent
This impious message. This virtuous,
Modest hypocrite has roused a whirlwind
In me, and for it she shall suffer. Go!
Bring her here before me—heed not her tears
Or prayers; bring her by force, if force should be
Required.

PRINCE CARSHENA.

One thought, most gracious sovereign,
We would suggest—Vashti is Queen,—as such,

Should be respected. Let not force be used,
To bring her here against her will,—manly,
Or king-like it would not appear.

> KING.

True! true! So long as she is Queen, she must
Be free from violence. We will not send
Again, but must here devise some proper
Mode of punishment. Pray tell me, Princes,
What shall be done with her, who wilfully
Has disobeyed the mandate of the King,
Insults our guests, and maligns the Princes
Of our realm?

> PRINCE MEMUCAN.

It gives me pain, O King!
To freely speak my mind respecting this
Domestic difficulty. Accomplished
Is the Queen, most wondrous fair, and doubtless
Is a noble lady, but like too many
Of her sex, she lacks discretion. She hath
A spirit, too,—which cannot brook control,—
Wild and ungoverned, and thus the counsels
Of the King she laughs to scorn, disobeys

His will, refuses to comply with his
Most just commands. The Sovereign's will is law,
And the King's dignity is public wealth,
In which all have an interest, and all
Must see preserved. The Nation's fame and power
Is founded on obedience, and he
Who disobeys, must be at heart a traitor.
Not thee alone, O King! hath Vashti wronged,
But all the nobles, princes and people
Throughout the provinces, for when abroad
'Tis whispered that " King Ahasuerus
Commanded Vashti the Queen, before him
To appear, but she came not," all women
Their husbands will despise, and the ladies
Of Media and Persia will likewise
Do, as did the Queen, and to their husbands
Show contempt.
          Therefore, if it please the King,
Let a decree go forth, and be written
Among the laws of Medes and Persians,—fixed,
And unalterable,—that " Queen Vashti
Be dethroned, and to another, better
Than she, be given her royal estate."

Throughout the empire let it be published,
That wives may honor give to those whose right
It is to claim it.

KING.

Most capital idea! Thy words
Do greatly please me, and it shall be done
Instanter. This proud Queen shall be dethroned,
Forfeited her estates, and to-morrow's
Sun shall see her crownless, kingless, banished
From the presence of her lord and master.
Yea; more! forthwith, into every province
Letters shall be sent, commanding every
Man to rule his household, and from his wife
Honor, and obedience to receive.

PRINCE ADMATHA.

Most just and righteous, are the decrees
Of our imperial master; but who
Will take the place of Vashti? The Sun
Must have its Venus, and the King his Queen.
If it please thee, most mighty Sovereign!
Throughout the provinces let officers
Be appointed, whose duty it shall be

Queen Esther. 41

To gather unto Shusan, all virgins
Fair and beautiful, and in the custody
Of the King's chamberlain let them be given
For purification. Let the King select
Therefrom—The one most pleasing in his sight
Shall then be Queen.

KING.

To me, Ahasuerus,
Was bequeathed this mighty empire, by my
Proud and noble ancestors. To preserve
Its laws, its power and glory, ever
Has been my strong desire, and though
My word is law, always have I consulted
The wishes of my people. Admatha's
Words meet my approval. I could at will,
Possess the wasting tenderness, the warm
Embraces of a thousand contending
Beauties; but 'tis proper that a worthy
Queen should be the sharer of my royal
Throne, and as such my honored wife. At once,
Officers will I appoint to gather
From near and distant provinces, virgins

Both beautiful and fair, and she who pleases
Best, shall be my Queen.   The feast is ended,
Let us retire.

(Exeunt.)

SCENE SECOND—IN A GLEN. MORDECAI ALONE.

MORDECAI. (*To himself.*)

How lonely, and how desolate
It seems, since Esther, my dear daughter, has
Become a Queen.   But a few months have passed,
And yet it seems an age,—so miserable,
And so wretched have I been.   I cannot
At home remain, for there no sparkling eyes,
No pleasant, joyous laughter, no loving
Kiss now greets me, but cold, dreary, cheerless
It appears, throwing a dark shadow thwart
My soul.   In this quiet spot, secluded
And alone,—by loiterers undisturbed,
I love to sit, and think of by-gone days;
Of Esther, as the little maid, unstained
By courtly honors.   Soon will she give me
Audience, as twice before she has done—

Most secretly, for the King knows not as yet
Her origin, or that she sprung from our
Cursed, Jewish race. She promised secrecy,
And I fear the anger of the King, should
He that fact discover.
     What a strange dream
Was that she told me—which I laughed to scorn,
And bade her to forget.—Dreamed she was lost,
Seized by an eagle, carried to his nest,
And 'mong the young eaglets brooded. All then
Was changed—the eagle was the King, eaglets
Were princes, the nest the palace Shushan,
And she the Queen. Ah! all! has proved most true.
Was it a vision of the future stamped
Upon her soul? did she not also dream
Of blessings to our race, and I honored
By the King? But hark! footsteps I hear!
And now I see approaching that villain
Bigthan, who, dog-like, hangs about the court;
A chamberlain, keeper of the King's door,
Who dared insult,—calling me a Jewish
Beggar. I would not meet him here, lest one
Should die, and on my hands I would not have

His blood. Within this hollow tree I will
Secrete myself, for with shrubbery its
Entrance is covered.

(Crowds into the hollow tree.)

(Enters Bigthan.)

BIGTHAN. *(To himself.)*

Teresh not here! 'Tis past the hour
Of meeting; on his promptness he always
Prides himself. How still this place, and quiet;
'Tis just the spot to lay our future plans,
And hatch up mischief. But here, in hot haste
He comes! like a blood-hound on its victim's
Tracks.

(Enter Teresh, another of the King's chamberlains.)

TERESH.

You here before me! It matters little
Who came first, since we are here, away from
All intruders. Look closely round,—be sure
No lurking spies are near, then let us quick
To business.

BIGTHAN.

My countenance is not villianous,
Nor do I thirst without cause for blood, but

When our brutal King so foully Vashti
Wronged, as her near kinsman I vowed revenge,
And oft I've felt inclined, into his breast
To plunge my dagger to its very hilt,
But my arm was stayed, for something whispered,
"*Wait a more convenient time.*" Die he must!
Soon will his pranks be ended, and Vashti
Be avenged.—Bigthan has sworn it, and his
Oath he holds inviolate.

TERESH.

                Our vows are mutual,
And oft I've felt like breaking o'er discretion's
Bounds, and in his very tracks slaying him,
Though for it my body in rusty chains
Might rot, or dangle by the hangman's rope,
Ignominiously from the gibbet.
Done secretly however, we are spared
All pain and degradation. Suggest some
Plan, by which safely, but effectively,
We can accomplish that we both desire.

BIGTHAN.

                If the dethroned Queen
He had restored to all her former rights,

And privileges, most cheerfully would
He have been forgiven. Esther he loves,
And to this new-found Goddess, to our shame,
Would sacrifice the glory of his throne,
Yea! the very life-blood of his loyal
Subjects. Who she is, he knows not, neither
Does he know her parentage, or lineage.
From obscurity she sprung, and 'tis said
She is a beggar's daughter,—whose pretty
Face has thus bewitched the King. It will end
In death, and that right speedily. You know
The secret door opening into corridors,
Dark and gloomy, leading to the narrow,
Tortuous stair-case, into subterranean
Vaults. In the farthest vault there can be found
A spring, just in the middle of the floor;
Firmly 'tis held by screws, but when unscrewed,
Wide open throws a trap-door, under which
Can be heard the rushing, surging, seething
Waters, flowing into the great cess-pool
Of the palace, and bottomless in depth.
      Of this secret door
I have the key, and at a stated hour,

Usually alone, the King passes it.
Behind the great pillar, near this door, you
Must be hid, with lasso all prepared. When
He comes, in homage will I bow, with words
" Your pardon, most mighty Sovereign," then quick
As lightning you must throw—standing behind—
The cord around his neck, thus strangling him,
And speechless, noiseless, through the corridors,
Down into the dark vaults, we'll drag him,
And when upon his knees he begs, and prays
For mercy, gently we'll slide his sacred
Majesty through this trap-door, down into
These fathomless waters, and like a dog
Will drown him.

TERESH.

Your scheme is well concocted,
And to the very letter it shall be
Carried out. Experts we are, in business
Such as this, and in this little play,—
Let it be comedy or tragedy,
Will act our parts most perfectly. When shall
The deed be done?

BIGTHAN.

  One week we give him yet to live.
Within that time, you must prepare the noose,
Made from the strongest cord, and 'twould be well
To practice throwing it. The vaults I'll visit,
And will have lights prepared, ready for use.
When seized, he must be strangled instantly,—
No groan, or cry escape him. When within
The secret door, not Heaven, nor Hell can
Save him.

TERESH.

  'Tis all arranged,—
Let us depart, we may be missed from court.

BIGTHAN.

  Agreed—Out of this place
We must be silent as the grave.

        (*Exeunt.*)

MORDECAI. (*Coming out of the tree.*)

  Consummate villains!
What horrors would they perpetrate upon
The King! Oh! how my blood ran cold, to hear
Them lay their devilish plans, their fiendish schemes.

Monsters they are in human form! In spirit,
They are devils! This moment I will go,
Claim audience of Esther, and to her
Disclose their schemes and purposes. The King
Shall yet be saved by me—the poor Jewish
Captive.
(Exit Mordecai.)

SCENE THIRD—QUEEN ESTHER'S APARTMENT IN THE PALACE.

QUEEN ESTHER. (*To herself.*)

Why are my spirits so depressed
To-day, surrounded as I am with proofs
Of tender love, and warmest sympathy?
Affectionate and kind, the King has ever
Been,—watching my footsteps with parental
Care, while across my pathway he throws his
Golden sunlight. Was my father with me,
Most happy should I be,—the throne would shine
More richly, and brighter sparkle the gems
Within my coronet. Thrice only have we met
Since I became a Queen. It seems an age
Since I last saw him,—but for a moment,

As spies, he said, were watching him, and 'twas
Dangerous for both. Could I tell the King
The story of my life, it might be well;
But this I cannot do, as faithfully
Have I promised secrecy. Come, cheer up!
Soon will I see him, and perhaps he will
Consent to what I may propose.

(Enter Ophelia, maid to Esther.)

OPHELIA.

There is, my royal Mistress,
In the ante-room, the man with whitened
Locks, named Mordecai, who thrice before has
Been admitted. He demands an audience
With the Queen.

QUEEN ESTHER.

He is an old friend,—
For years we have been acquainted. Show him
All due respect whenever he shall call.
Invite him in.

(Exit Ophelia.)

MORDECAI. *(Entering, and embracing her.)*

Thank heaven! again we meet;
What mean these tears?

QUEEN ESTHER.

Tears flow from joy,
As well as sorrow. I am so happy
When I see you, that I must weep. But come,
Sit down, for weary you appear. Is it
Well with thee?

MORDECAI.

Well as usual,
But have come on business,—most imperative,
And time must not be wasted.

QUEEN ESTHER.

You frighten me!
Your words forebode some evil.

MORDECAI.

How in the human breast do passions rage,
When once let loose, and from their proper bounds
Are free. How madly do they onward rush,
Swift as the fierce tornado, up-rooting
All those noble gifts, which God has planted
In the soul. Dark, proud, suspicious, brooding
O'er their hate, and by the basest passions
Led, two chamberlains of the King,—on duty

In the palace, have sworn to take his life,
And schemes most villainous have they laid, to take
Him unawares, and to a bottomless
Pit consign him.

QUEEN.

What! Murder the King!
It cannot, cannot be!—still, you would not
Deceive me thus?

MORDECAI.

Sooner would I take my life,
Than cause a needless pang, or crush your heart,
Pure and sensitive as it is, by words
Too horrible to relate.—*It is true.*

QUEEN ESTHER.

As mist of morning shadows earth,
So has my mind, by a dark cloud, all day
Been over-cast. It was inexplicable—
Something I could not understand; therefore
I charged it to thine absence, and the want
Of thy dear companionship, which I have
Thought of, dreamed of, and anxiously desired.

But hasten! tell me of the plot, and who
These blood-hounds are, who thirst for royal blood.

MORDECAI.

When Vashti was dethroned,
To many it gave offence, 'mong whom were
The two chamberlains, Bigthan and Teresh,
Her kinsmen, and keepers of the palace
Doors. This morning, as of late has been my
Custom, I visited a quiet spot,—
A glen, which lieth towards the east, to think
Of thee, my Esther, for thou art ever
Present in my mind. While there, Bigthan
I saw approaching—the man whose insults
I have borne—and, wishing to avoid him,
Betook myself into a great hollow
Tree, there standing. Soon Teresh came—his name
Was spoken, and I knew his voice—and then
They swore revenge, and laid their murderous plans
To waylay, and destroy the King. I heard
Them all, for near the tree they stood, wherein
Concealed and undiscovered I remained.
One week they spare the King,—
Then all prepared, when he shall come alone,

Passing the secret door, leading to vaults
Beneath the palace, Bigthan is to bow,
And say, " Your pardon, most mighty Sovereign,"
Thus gaining the attention of the King,
While Teresh, secreted by the great pillar
Standing near the door, as quick as lightning,
From behind darts out, and throws a rope-noose
Round the King's neck, thus strangling him,—then
    through
The secret door, and corridors, they are
To drag him down to the lowest, farthest
Vault, and headlong cast him into waters,
Deep, and bottomless.

              QUEEN ESTHER.
           Oh, horrible!
The thought is sickening! How shall we act
To save the King, and give these human fiends
Their just deserts?

              MORDECAI.
            You must obtain at once,
An audience with the King: then tell him
All. At a moment's notice, I shall be
Ready to appear, and verify my

Charges. But Esther, I forget I am
A Jew, and that my word may not avail
Against the oaths of villains, standing high
In office. Tell him some strategy to use,—
Some secret method, whereby my words may
Be confirmed. Doubtless there is a secret
Passage to the vaults, from inner chamber,—
Through this the King might pass some chosen
    guards,
And in the darkened corridors conceal
Them. Let him have prepared, collar of steel
To wear about his neck, and guards near by
Secreted, to watch, and guard his person
When they spring upon him. Great secrecy
Should be used, lest they his plans discover,
And adopt some other scheme,—failing
In this.

              QUEEN ESTHER.
           Your counsels are most wise,
And with the King, my influence I'll exert
For their adoption. Now, fare thee well, my
Best of fathers!—but accept this little
Token of your Esther's love.

                        (Offering a purse.)

MORDECAI.

No! No!—I need not gold, but seek alone
My Esther's happiness. One kiss I'll take,
And then depart. May Heaven guard thee, child!
And on thee, shower her richest blessings.

(Exeunt.)

ACT III.

SCENE FIRST—HAMAN IN THE OUTWARD COURT OF THE PALACE.

HAMAN. (*To himself.*)

Am I not Haman!
Respected by the King, and standing high
Above all other princes of the realm?
Am I not petted, toadied by the court,
While servants bow, and do me reverence—
As if to royalty? My rank is now
Exalted, and next to the King I stand
The idol of the people. With wishes
Gratified, most proudly could I exult,
Were I not scorned, despised by Mordecai,
Who, sitting in the King's gate, throws on me
A most contemptuous smile, and will not
Bow, and do me homage. Not he alone,
But the whole Jewish race, now imitate
His clownish manners, which tend to blast my
Honor, and traduce my fame. Mordecai

Shall die!—and with him, all the Jews throughout
The provinces shall be destroyed; none shall
Be spared—not even the women, nor young
And helpless children. I will see the King
At once; will before him lay this vital
Matter, and press it to an issue. Here
Comes the King's chamberlain.

CHAMBERLAIN.

His Majesty, the King,
Bids you come in.

HAMAN.

(Entering the inner apartment, bows, and salutes the King.)

Health, and long life,
Most gracious Sovereign.

KING.

What is the wish
Of my most faithful servant?

HAMAN.

In all the provinces of the kingdom,
Imperial Master!—scattered among
The people, are a race of Jews, head-strong,
Envious, and bigoted, who glory

In their shame, violating enactments
Thou hast made, trampling on laws, and boldly
Thy mandates disobeying. Their manners,
Customs, laws, diverse from ours, will ever
Urge them in the forbidden ways, which lead
To rank disloyalty. We have done all
That could be done, this evil to correct,
But 'tis in vain! Our words are treated
With disdain, and hurled into our faces
Back, with cold, contemptuous scorn. Actions
Like these will tell on others. Flame, begets
Flame, so disloyalty begets her kind.
If it please thee, O King! let a decree
Go forth for their destruction.—Accomplish
This, then in the King's treasury I will
Pay of silver, one thousand talents.

KING.
    The silver
To thee is given, the people also,—
Do with them, as in thy sight seemeth good.
Let the scribes be called, and writings at once
Prepared, even as thou shall dictate. Let
Them to governors and rulers be sent

Throughout the provinces, and in all tongues
And languages published—" That on the thirteenth
Day, of the twelfth month, all Jews of every.
Age and sex, women and little children,
Old and young, shall be destroyed." Take this ring,
And with it, seal the writings.—The King has
Thus decreed, in his palace Shushan,
(Gives the ring.)

HAMAN.

It shall be done O King! their doom is sealed,—
They die! This most presumptuous race, shall know
There is a power supreme, that will enforce
Obedience to thy will.—I hasten
To do thy bidding.
(Exeunt.)

SCENE SECOND.—THE QUEEN'S APARTMENT.

Queen Esther—Ophelia and Bashmah her maids.

OPHELIA.

Pardon, my Royal Mistress!
I permission crave, to speak of one whom

You respect, and whom you bade me honor
As your friend.

QUEEN ESTHER.

    You have permission.
Speak freely, for of my friends, I always
Love to hear.

OPHELIA.

'Tis of him called Mordecai;
For passing through the palace a moment
Since, before the King's gate I saw him clothed
In sackcloth, and with ashes covered. Loud,
And bitter was the cry by him sent forth,
As of some dire calamity. I know
Not what it means, but surely some great grief
Must be upon him.

BASHMAH.

   Your Majesty will give me leave to say
I also saw him, and others there were,
Weeping and wailing, and like him were clothed
In sackcloth.

QUEEN ESTHER.

Mordecai, in sackcloth clothed!
God forbid, that on him any evil
Should have fallen! Hasten at once Ophelia;
Call my attendant Hatach,—bid him come
Instantly to the Queen's presence.

(Exit Ophelia.)

What can have happened? this doubt and painful
Fear, pierces my very soul, and makes me
Sick at heart. Oh! how it throbs! and the blood
Seems rushing to my brain.

BASHMAH.

Fear not my Royal Mistress!—it may be
For some friend lost, or for some other thing
Which little concerns your majesty;
But here comes Hatach.

(Hatach entering and bowing.)

HATACH.

The royal summons I obey.
Pray tell me your commands.

QUEEN ESTHER.

Mordecai you know? he, who sitteth
Almost daily, in the King's gate. Before
The gate you'll find him now, in sackcloth clothed,—
Hasten at once, and to him say you have
A message from the Queen; that she desires
The sackcloth taken from him, and other
Raiment has she sent in place thereof. Treat
Him most gently, and no language use, harsh,
Or impertinent. Yea, more! say to him,
"The Queen desires to know the cause thereof,
And why he weeps and wails, and putteth on
This badge of mourning." Disclose to no one
But myself the message he may send me.
Now hasten quickly! and I will count
The moments of your absence.

HATACH.

Adieu! my gracious Queen,—
Nothing thou desirest, shall be left
Undone.

(Exit Hatach.)

QUEEN ESTHER.

You can retire Ophelia,—
You also Bashmah to the ante-room,
As I would be alone. Show Hatach in,
Soon as he returns. Have no delay.

(Exeunt Ophelia and Bashmah.)

QUEEN ESTHER. *(To herself.)*

Most mysterious
Are the ways of Providence!—Yesterday,
It was all sun-light, o'er my path; to-day,
The storm-clouds gather, and darkness covers
Me. Some evil, like a thunder-bolt, has
Fallen on my dear, kind father. What can
It be?—Some matter serious, I fear; not for
A trivial cause would he act thus. Music
Is discord, and the blazing sun is dark
When heart is clouded. None but a daughter's
Heart can know a daughter's sorrows, when a loved
Father suffers. The time I trust will come,
When I can have him with me, to comfort,
And to strengthen him. For this I daily
Pray, and something whispers that my prayer will

Yet be answered. God grant it may be so.
Soon shall I know all;. my faithful Hatach
Has a tender heart, and my father knows
Full well how I esteem him. I must dry
These tears which have so freely flowed, must cleanse
My eyes, so red from weeping, for Hatach
Soon will come,—to hear the worst, must be
Prepared.

OPHELIA. *(Entering.)*

My Honored Mistress,—Hatach has arrived.
Shall I admit him?

QUEEN ESTHER.

Yes; bid him come in.

HATACH. *(Entering and bowing.)*

My Sovereign Mistress! Mordecai I found
In sackcloth, and to him your message was
Delivered. He told me all, how the King
By Haman influenced, had decreed the death
Of all the Jews throughout the provinces,
Sparing neither old nor young, women nor
Little children. 'Tis on the thirteenth day,

Of the twelfth month, that this evil will be
Consummated. This writing, he bade me
Give you,—'tis a copy of the decree,
Made by the King, in his palace Shushan.

(Gives her the decree.)

QUEEN ESTHER.

Destroy the Jews,
Sparing neither old nor young!--Horrible!
What can it mean? It is the King's decree,
And bears his seal, but why such madness?

HATACH.

Haman was wroth and envious, because
Mordecai bowed not, nor did him homage
As do others. Against the Jews, the King's
Ear he poisoned, making them appear an
Envious, bigoted, disloyal race,
Who the laws violated, and at naught
Set the King's commands. Strongly, he urged their
Death, and silver offered—one thousand talents
Into the King's treasury to be paid,
When 'twas accomplished.

QUEEN ESTHER.

Most infamous Haman!
Pride, envy, malice, and revengeful hate
Against our Jewish race, doth fill his heart,
Which, in the blood of Innocents he would
Satiate. His chosen people, God has,
And will preserve, spite of the ambitious
Pride of him, who has disgraced the laurels
By the King conferred. He is a traitor!
And deserves a traitor's fate.—But this dire
Calamity ; how shall it be avoided?

HATACH.

Mordecai advised,
That you at once should go in unto the King,
And supplication make in their behalf.
Your prayers, and warm entreaties, might yet
Avert the doom, now hanging o'er them.

QUEEN ESTHER.

To do this seems impossible.
For thirty days last past, into the presence
Of the King, have I not been called, and all

The people know, that whosoever shall
Come unto the King, within the inner
Court uncalled, either man, or woman, shall
Be put to death. Such is the law, and none
Are spared, excepting such, to whom the King
Extends the golden sceptre.

HATACH.

Such is the law
Of Media and Persia. To Mordecai
I stated it, who fully understands
Its meaning, and its penalties. But yet
He sent this message. "Go tell the Queen" said
He, "that if this evil comes upon the Jews,
She must not think in the King's palace
To escape. If she holds her peace, safety
And deliverance to the Jews, surely
Shall from another quarter come, but she,
And all her father's house, shall be destroyed."

QUEEN ESTHER.

Did he say this? then will I go, let come
What may. Hasten now, and to Mordecai

Bear this message. "Go gather all the Jews
In Shushan now residing, and with them
Fast ye for me, and for three days, neither
Eat nor drink.—I, with my maidens, likewise
Will fast, and then contrary to the law
Will I go in unto the King; and if
I perish,—I perish."

HATACH.

    Most faithfully,
Thy message shall be delivered.

(Exit Hatach.)

QUEEN ESTHER. *(To herself.)*

  I wake, as from some frightful dream!
Vashti, for disobedience was dethroned,
And for the same, I may be executed.
O shame! O infamy! this cursed envenom'd
Malice, this proud insolence of Haman,
Doth scald my eyes with tears, and in my soul,
Opens new veins of torture.—But courage
Take! There is a power unseen, that rules
The destinies of nations, that will plunge
From gulf to gulf,—from shame to deeper shame,

This incarnate fiend, who would our Jewish
Race destroy. 'Tis the same power that closed
The lion's mouth, and kept from harm our prophet
Daniel, when in their frightful den, headlong
He was thrown.—Prayer, I will offer.

(She kneels and prays.)

" O Thou ! great King of Kings, and Lord of Lords !
Omnipotent and Omnipresent ! Thou
Dost ever hear the feeblest whisperings
Of those, who put their trust in Thee. Before
Thee bows Thine hand maid, who, into Thine heart
Of love, would pour her griefs and sorrows. Her
Feeble mind, strengthen and support, and with
A will, fixed and determined, let her Thy
Purposes perform. When before the King
Uncalled she goes, into her mouth put fit
And proper words, that she may plainly, boldly
Speak as doth become his Queen. Let her not
Utterance give to thoughts which may displease,
Or to him, seem presumptuous, or improper.
Soften the King's heart, and toward Thine handmaid,

Make it tender, that in his sight, she may
Find favor. Above all things, O Thou, great
Jehovah! preserve thy chosen people,
And to the King, disclose the vile designs
Of proud Haman's heart, and the great evil
Impending o'er our race. In Thee, we trust,
And to Thy care, commit ourselves.—Amen."

SCENE THIRD.—INNER COURT OF KING'S PALACE.

The King upon his throne, and Esther waiting opposite him in the court. She is seen by the King, who extends to her his golden sceptre, thus inviting her to approach him—She obeys and advances.

QUEEN ESTHER. (*To herself.*)

Thank Heaven!—
With pleased, approving smile, the King doth look
Upon me, and now his golden sceptre
He extends, thus bidding me in safety
To approach. I will at once advance.

(*She approaches the King, and touches the sceptre.*)

KING.

As the dove flies to her nest,
So comes my Queenly Esther to her liege

Lord, who, a most hearty welcome gives her.
Though absent, most frequently have I thought
Of thee, and but a moment since, when free
From the engrossing cares which try and vex
The soul, my restless mind went wandering back
To that bright-eyed Goddess, who has ever
Warmed, and cheered my heart, even, when with
    clouds,
And darkness 'twas o'ershadowed. To what kind
Fortune do I owe this visit?—Esther
Could not think I had forgotten, or had
Deserted her, for oftimes have I said,
"The King must not encroach too often on
Her privacy."

QUEEN ESTHER.

    Most fully does the Queen appreciate,
The kind regards, and noble sentiments
Of the King. Accept, most mighty Sovereign!
Your Esther's thanks, for the tender treatment,
The warm love, you have ever manifested,—
For the many blessings strewn so thickly
Along her pathway, making her life-days,

So joyous, and so happy. To preserve
Thy throne, thy life, thy happiness, freely
Would I sacrifice my own.

KING.

What! is there some secret
Plot against my Kingdom, or my life? Once,
I remember, thou didst such plot reveal,
When Bigthan with Teresh foully conspired
To seize, and strangle ; then, to the vaults consign
Me. Caught in the act by timely warning,
They from the gibbet swung.—Thou, Esther didst
Save my life.

QUEEN ESTHER.

Another saved it !—even Mordecai,
The Jew. But enough of this ; no foul plot
Against the King exists, for he is blessed
Beyond the reach of fear. The Queen has come,
Simply to crave a favor from the King.

KING.

What is thy wish Queen Esther?
What wilt thou have? speak; for it shall be given,
Even to the half of my Kingdom.

QUEEN ESTHER.

If in thy sight, O King!
Favor I have found,—if it shall please thee,
To listen to my prayer, and my request
Perform, then come to-morrow, and with you
Bring Haman to the banquet, which I shall
Have prepared, and then, and there, all the King
Desires will I do, and to thee, present
My humble petition.

KING.

'Twill give us both great pleasure,
To meet you at the banquet.—Most gladly
I accept, and will be there with Haman.

QUEEN ESTHER.

The King is very kind;—
With a light heart I leave his presence, with
Certainty of meeting him to-morrow.
Adieu, most gracious Sovereign!—Heaven bless you!

KING.

Heaven bless my lovely Queen,
And may kind Angels guard, protect her.—
Adieu!

(Exit Esther.)

Queen Esther.

(To himself.)

How charmingly she looked!—what a sweet smile
Lit up her features when gazing on me,
As if to read my very soul. Innocent,
And thoughtful she has ever been; faultless,
And free from guile. What is it she desires?
Something of moment, else within this court
She would not have appeared. It matters not:—
Nothing I could refuse her. A message
I will send at once to Haman, bidding
Him to meet me at the banquet, for she
Desires his presence. Perhaps for him,
She'll ask some higher honor.

SCENE FOURTH.—HAMAN'S RESIDENCE.

Haman, Zeresh his Wife and Friends.

HAMAN.

With fortune, and with honor,
Have I been crowned. Next to the King I stand,
And with him share all regal honors. From
This high pinnacle of fame, on Princes,

And on petty Kings, can I look down, and bid
Them come, and go, like abject slaves. The King
Himself, my will performs; he daily comes,
Consults me, takes my advice, and ever
Does as I propose. In vain do malice,
Envy, hate, attempt to tear the laurels
From Haman's brow;—above their blasting
Reach, they will securely thrive and flourish.
The King has ever been my warmest friend,
And now the Queen seeks my companionship.
From her a message I received, asking
My presence at her banquet. To-morrow
The King, and I alone attend.—Perhaps
Some favor she would grant, or love itself
May burn within her bosom,—if so,
I will possess it.
    One thought however,
Like a dagger pierces my heart, and drives
Me to despair. Of what avail are wealth,
And honors, so long as Mordecai the Jew
Sitteth in the King's gate?—with scorn, and cold
Contempt, doth frown upon me as I pass,
And will not bow, or do me reverence.

But to-day, this base, ungrateful, haughty
Wretch, lost to all sense of shame and common
Decency, did spit his vemon at me
As I passed ;—like a huge reptile, did he
Glare upon me. He would not move, or stir,
But on me showered his insults, silent, but
Most contemptible, and by all noticed.

ZERESH.

This insolent, audacious man,
Perverse and obstinate, whose pride is past
Endurance, should be taught, what others now
Have learned—good manners to their superiors.
Why not seize the wretch, and flay him publicly,
'Till on bended knees, he sues for mercy?

HAMAN.

Half inclined was I to do it,
But something stayed me—street brawls I like not,
But to myself I swore revenge.—My time
Will come.

A FRIEND.

The time has come!
Delays are dangerous; this vile Jewish

Dog, should at once be taught to know his master,
For give him but a chance, and he will add
New insults to his hate.

SECOND FRIEND.

I would advise
That he be strangled; hung! Let it be done
Publicly,—'twill have on others, a good
Effect.

ZERESH.

The thought is timely; in a public spot
Let gallows be erected: let it be
In height some fifty cubits, and thereon
Let Mordecai be hung. Speak to the King
Concerning it, and then unto the banquet,
Thou shalt go most merrily.

HAMAN.

Great satisfaction would it give,
And well does he deserve it. Orders will
I give, and this very day, the gallows
Fifty cubits high, shall be erected,—.
Not in a public place, but in the court

Of mine own house, and as the King liveth,
Mordecai shall hang thereon. To-morrow,
Early in the day, the Sovereign I will
See, and his consent obtain ; then, without
Delay shall he be executed.

ZERESH.

My lord most wisely speaks ;
Let him proceed—the work complete.

FRIEND.

Of the plan proposed,
Most fully we approve. This gross insult
To our lord, in blood must be wiped out.

HAMAN.

More freely can I breathe, when he is dead.
I know not how it is, but his destiny
Seems linked with mine, and while living, I fear
And hate him—when dead, my vengence will be
Satisfied, and my joy and peace restored.
But haste me !—let us lose no time, for we
Must be prepared.

(Exeunt.)

ACT IV.

SCENE FIRST—PALACE SHUSHAN.

Private apartment of the King.

KING. (*To himself.*)

Something is wrong!—
A sleepless night I've passed, tossing upon
My bed like a frightened infant. What means
This mystery,—this most strange behavior
Of my senses, this mist that hangs about
My soul? What means this power invisible;
This mysterious influence that thrills
My heart, and makes me shudder? Oh! how I've
Tossed and moaned in troubled sleep like a sick
Child! how slowly the hours have crept along;
The night has seemed an age of misery.
I feel, I must confess a sense of shame,
And blush at my own weakness, so unlike
My usual nature. Restless, timorous,
Nervous, with no apparent cause, I saw

Those airy shadows, spectral visions, which
" Like bubbles, big with emptiness alone,
Burst and vanished into nothingness." Like
Melting smoke that mingles with the sky, before
Me they flitted for a moment,—then quickly
Disappeared. One short dream I had, and on
My mind it seems distinctly stamped. Methought
A maiden kneeled before me; beautiful
She was, her shoulders covered o'er with her
Disheveled tresses, and her large, lustrous
Eyes suffused with tears. In piteous tones
She pleaded for her father's life,—a grey-
Haired man, who kneeled beside her—told of his
Wrongs and sufferings, and how by malice
And revenge, to death he had been condemned.
Most earnestly she pleaded—urged that he,
In time gone by, had saved my life and crown,
When against them traitors had conspired.
    She looked like Esther,
So fair and beautiful—her large, black eyes
Expressing her very thoughts. I was about
To speak, and ask them who they were, but then
Awoke, and all had vanished. Again,

I dropped asleep, and frightful visions saw
Of scaffolds, with all their gloomy trappings,
And above them all, went towering one huge
Gallows, beneath which, stood the grey-haired man,
With rope about his neck, for execution.
To save him, I started up! but awoke
To find myself alone, and the cold drops
Of perspiration, covering my forehead.
     'Tis morning now,
And the bright sun has risen, dispelling
Shadows and night-mists from the earth, but not
The dream-clouds from my mind. May be
Some great injustice has been done. Laid up
In archives, are records of chronicles
Made by my scribes; they shall be brought before
Me, and thoroughly examined. Perhaps
They will reveal the cause of my distress.
Ho! my attendants.

    (*Enter Mehumen the chamberlain, bowing.*)

KING.

Go, call my scribe, and with him bring
The book of Records.—Make no delay.

MEHUMEN.

It shall be done, O King!
As thou commandest.

(Exit Mehumen.)

KING. *(To himself.)*

Ever, my thoughts revert to Esther;
'Tis to-day we banquet with her—my heart
Should not be clouded, nor my mind perplexed.
If in the Records, no strange thing is found,
Then, at once I'll drive these fearful night-thoughts
From my mind—with smiling face and joyous
Heart, her banquet will attend—to her soul,
I will not bring disquietude.

(Enter Mehumen and scribe with book of Records.)

KING. *(To the scribe.)*

Look o'er the Records, and see
If can be found, a person, who has done
Great service to the King, respecting whom,
Some special mention, recently has been
Made.

SCRIBE. (*Examining the Records.*)

We find here written, most gracious Sovereign !
As follows: "In the sixth year, of the reign
Of Ahasuerus, whose proud Empire
Extendeth from India even unto
Ethiopia, two chamberlains, servants
Of the King, by name Bigthan and Teresh,
Wilfully and maliciously conspired
Against the Crown, Kingdom, and the King's life,
And sought secretly, to seize and strangle
Our mighty Sovereign, and to the lowest
Vault consign him. Let it be remembered,
That to one Mordecai, the Jew, the thing
Became known, who, to the Queen the vile plot
Disclosed, and she, to the King revealed it.
By a strategem proposed by Mordecai,
These villains in the very act were seized,
Condemned, and on the gibbet executed.
To Mordecai, the Jew, belongeth honor."

KING.

For these most loyal acts,
What honor, or what dignity has been
Conferred on Mordecai?

MEHUMEN

None whatever!—He still is sitting
In the King's Gate.

SCRIBE.

No mention here is made
Of anything, by which he was rewarded.

KING.

Go at once Mehumen;—see whom you find
Standing in the outward court.

MEHUMEN.

Haman alone is there, waiting
For an audience with the King.

KING.

Bid him come in.

(Exit Mehumen.)

(Enter Haman who had come to speak unto the King to hang Mordecai on the gallows prepared.)

KING. *(To Haman.)*

There is one, who unto us great service
Hath performed, and on him, we would bestow

Most royal favors.   What shall now be done
To him, whom the King delighteth to honor?

   HAMAN.   (*Thinking the King referred to himself.*)

    I would not most mighty Sovereign!
Appear presumptuous ; but the man on whom
Thou wouldst bestow Imperial honors,
And in whose dignities thou dost delight
Thyself, should be clothed, as might well become
The King's favorite.   Let be brought royal
Apparel, thou hast worn ; the Niscan horse
Brought from Armenia,—the favorite steed,
Which the King rideth,—and the Crown Royal.
Into the hands of noble Princes, let
Them be delivered, to array the man
Thus honored by the King, and through the streets
Of the city, let him be borne on horseback,
With Princes in attendance, who before
Him shall proclaim—"thus, shall be done to him,
Whom the King delighteth to honor."

     KING.

  Well spoken Haman!—make thee haste;
Take the apparel, crown, and horse, as thou

Hast said, so do to Mordecai, the Jew,
Who, at the King's gate, you will find sitting ;—
Of all thou hast spoken, let nothing fail ;
The King would honor him above all others.
In person, do thou attend him, and make
The proclamation.

HAMAN.

Thy Sovereign will must be obeyed,—
I go, and do thy bidding.

(Exit Haman.)

SCENE SECOND—QUEEN ESTHER'S PRIVATE APARTMENTS.

The King—Esther the Queen, and Haman at the banquet.

KING.

'Tis pleasant thus to throw off cares,—
Vexatious cares, the wormwood and the gall,
Which so embitter life. Like opiates
In a fever, these social gatherings
Quiet the nerves, and cool the heated
Brain, inducing rest, and quietude
Of mind.

QUEEN ESTHER.

    Indeed ! great joy it gives,
To know, that I have added to the King's
Happiness. Ever would I fill his heart
With pleasant, happy thoughts, as sky is filled
With sunbeams, and earth with shining rivulets.

KING.

    But Esther, of thine own happiness,
Have you no thought?

QUEEN ESTHER.

    Of myself, I have but little thought
Except to serve my God, and please my King.
Let them but smile upon me, I am as
Happy as the joyous bird, which warbles
Its notes of praise, when the bright sun sends forth
Its laughing beams, at early dawn.

KING.

    Of thy petition
I would know, and thy request. Didst thou not
Promise, at the banquet to present them?

I am now, as then, prepared to grant them,
Even to the half of my Kingdom.

QUEEN ESTHER.

If in thy sight, O King!
Thine Esther hath favor found; if it shall
Please thee, to grant her prayer, know thou, O King!
I am a Jewess!—one of the daughters
Of that noble, but persecuted race,
Who though despised, and trodden under foot,
Are still most loyal subjects. We are sold!—
Myself, and people—not as bond-women,
And bond-men, for then in silence would have
Suffered, and no complaint have made, but we
Are doomed to death—to be destroyed and slain,
Guiltless and crimeless. Spare my life, and lives
Of all my people!—this, O King! is my
Petition.

KING.

Thy words are riddles!
What secret plot would you unravel? Lives
There a wretch so base, as would desire
Thy death, or even dream of thy destruction?

Who, and where is he, who in his inmost
Heart, hath cherished such a thought?

QUEEN ESTHER.

Now seated with us at the banquet,
Is the vile plotter of this scheme for our
Destruction.   Look thou, O King! on Haman,
Sitting like senseless marble,—See his face
O'erspread with ashy paleness; the painful
Terror in his eye; his tongue suspended;
His trembling form, and guilt so strongly stamped
On every feature of his countenance.
He is the man!—the enemy, who plots
This evil 'gainst the Queen, and all her race.

KING.

'Tis true! the perjured slave! the traitorous
Villain, in every form and manner shows
His guilt.   Excuse me for a moment: into
The garden I must retire, my heated
Brain to cool, and thoughts collect.   He shall have
His just deserts.

(Exit King.)

HAMAN.

(Rising up, and falling on his knees before the Queen, who was seated on a couch.)

Here at thy feet, pardon I crave
Most Honored Mistress!—O spurn me not!
Have pity on a wretch, who now with shame,
Doth make confession of his sins, and begs
Thy kind forgiveness. Oh! let these scalding
Tears so freely flowing, wash out my crimes,
And evil purposes, and ever will
I be, your abject slave.

QUEEN ESTHER.

Touch me not! thou prince of villians!—
By thy vile breath, I would not be foully
Contaminated.

HAMAN.

Oh! spare my life! speak to the King,
For there was evil in his eye, and death
Will be my doom, unless thou dost secure
My pardon. Do but this, and at thy feet,
Worm-like I'll ever crawl.—Make me thy slave.

(He falls upon the couch by her side just as the King enters.)

KING.

What do I see!—Before me,
In the palace, would he force the Queen?—
Ho! my attendants.

(Enter Harbonah and other chamberlains.)

Let him be covered, for to death he is
Condemned.

(They cover Haman's face.)

HARBONAH.

Most mighty Sovereign! In Haman's house
There stands a gallows, in height some fifty
Cubits. 'Twas made by Haman, and thereon
He would have hung Mordecai, had the King
Consented. 'Tis all prepared, with scaffold,
And with trappings, and at a moment's notice
Can be used.

KING.

Then seize the villain! bear him hence, and like
A dog hang him thereon! Upon his head
Let fall, the mischief by him conceived.

HARBONAH.

It shall be done, O King!—
Quickly, as thou commandest.

(They seize Haman and bear him out to execution.)

SCENE THIRD—THE QUEEN'S APARTMENT IN THE PALACE.

Queen Esther and Mordecai.

QUEEN ESTHER.

Welcome! thrice welcome to my heart and home,
My dear, good father! Let me embrace thee,
Kiss thee, as I was wont to do, when coming
From your daily toil, I ran to meet you
With a kiss of love—in your loving
Arms so tenderly was held, while calling
Me your "*darling little pet.*" How all has
Changed, since in that humble, quiet home, we
Lived together! all but our hearts—they will
Always burn with love and pure affection,
Will they not?

MORDECAI.

   As a little maid, thou wast my pride
And joy; and now the crown of womanhood,
Which shines untarnished. With fond affection
Thy welcome I return, and the parental
Kiss, most willingly I give my Esther.
Yes! we have somewhat changed;—you, from the
  young,
Romping girl, who played among the flowers,
And chased the butterflies, to the majestic
Queen, and I, the despised and persecuted
Jew, have now become the King's favorite,
Wearing the royal robes, and classed
Among his Nobles. Let me but go forth,
On every side fawning, bowing, cringing,
Are the fops and sycophants of court, who, like
Dastard Knaves, would honor me as Master.
I like them not, but scorn, despise them now,
As they once did me.

QUEEN ESTHER.

   When last you saw the King,
What did he say?

MORDECAI.

I saw him but a moment since ;
Said he,—"go in, and see the Queen, your daughter."
I was about to speak, but he continued—
"She has told me all,—go in, and I will
Meet you there." His words were most ambiguous,
But kindly spoken. But tell me Esther,
Have you made known our near relationship,
Or elsewhere has he learned it?

QUEEN ESTHER.

I have told him all!—
To him, have I revealed the inmost secrets
Of my heart. He knows your love and kindness
To the poor orphan child, and the strong cords
Of love, that bind our hearts together. He
Even knows the dream you bid me to forget,
But now, as fresh within my mind, as if
But yesterday I dreamed it.

MORDECAI.

I do remember it!—'Twas a strange dream ;
Most marvelous it should have come to pass
Just as it has. Esther, thou hast blest our

Race, or rather thou hast been God's chosen
Instrument to do it. To Jehovah,
Our thanks are ever due ; to His Great Name,
Be all the praise and glory.—But the King
Cometh !

(The King enters.)

QUEEN ESTHER.

    Welcome, our gracious Sovereign !—
For thy royal presence, accept our thanks,
And grateful homage. Thou hast crowned our lives
With gladness, and from our hearts hast driven
Sorrow. Most precious in our sight, is the King's
Life and happiness.

KING.

And in our lovely Queen, is the King's life
Bound up. Thy happiness is mine, and all
That is mine, is thine. But now to business.
Haman, thine enemy is dead—his sons
Are also dead, and to thee, Queen Esther
Do I give his house, and vast possessions.
They are thine ; use them as thou deemest best.

QUEEN ESTHER.

Language cannot express, O King!
The feelings of my heart, for these continued
Favors. The gift is precious—most precious,
Since it comes from thee.

KING.

Some fit, and proper person
You should select, who, in your name and place,
Will have the charge and management of this
House, and vast estate.—To my mind, no one
So fit and suitable as your father,
Mordecai.

QUEEN ESTHER,

You do surprise me, most agreeably!
Thanks, O King! for this thy wise selection.
With thy kind permission, I do hereby
Appoint my father, Mordecai, to rule
This house of Haman, and over his lands
And large possessions place him. May he be
Wise, discreet, and ever live the faithful
Servant of the king.

MORDECAI.

Accept most noble Sovereign, and you my
Queen, the homage of your servant. The trusts
To me confided, ever will I hold
Most sacred, and perform them to the best
Of my ability.

KING.

To the place of Haman, we have advanced
Thee, Mordecai. Next to the King, thou standest
In authority. We would have thee clothed
In royal robes of blue and white, with crown
Of gold, and with garments of fine linen
And purple, that the city of Shushan
May rejoice and be glad. Now take this ring
With royal seal—token of thy power,
And with it seal the writings you may send
In the King's name to all the Jews, scattered
Throughout the provinces, even from India
Unto Ethiopia, and to the rulers
Thereof, commanding to gather themselves
Together, armed and prepared to destroy
And slay, all who may assault them. All legal
Rights, thy Jewish people, hereafter must

Queen Esther.

And shall enjoy, for no man can reverse
These writings, in the King's name prepared,
And with this ring sealed. Now go! let the scribes
At once prepare writings you may dictate,
And with all speed, let them be sent by posts
On horseback, into the one hundred, twenty-
Seven provinces of our Kingdom.

MORDECAI.

Thy Sovereign will, O King! shall be performed,
And thy decrees, this very day shall be
Sent forth throughout the Realm. Again accept
My thanks and homage.
                                            (*Exit Modecai bowing.*)

QUEEN ESTHER. (*To the King.*)

      Oh! what a royal heart
Thou doth possess Heaven must have inspired
These manly thoughts, induced thee to perform
These noble acts, which, in the Chronicles
Of Ages shall be recorded. Millions
Yet unborn, shall to their children recount
The virtues of the good King Ahasuerus.—

Yes! posterity shall praise thee, and ages
Yet to come, record thy goodness.

KING.

Heaven has greatly blessed,
By giving me an angel for a Queen,
And she has taught me goodness, if within
It can be found. Like stars which shine forever,
So shine thy virtues in the firmament
Of my being, and if in future ages
My name is mentioned, it will only be
As linked with thine, my ESTHER.

LOVE AND TRUST.

From "Demorest's Weekly," by permission.

Lessons of Life.

A COLLOQUIAL POEM.

LESSONS OF LIFE.

SCENE I.

SPIRIT FROM ANOTHER PLANET.

ABOVE THE EARTH.—MORNING.

SPIRIT.

How beautiful the earth ! the rising Sun
Like a huge fire-ball, reddens the eastern
Sky, tinging the horizon as if with
Burnished gold. Onward, he moves in glory !
Scattering from vale to mountain top, his
Dazzling beams, to active duty calling
Old and young—on all bestowing favors.
Blest Almoner of the All Wise ! All Good !
All Powerful ! new life thou dost impart
To all who feel thy presence ; the barren
Rock now smiles, while for joy the hill-sides laugh,
Because thou deignest to stoop, and kiss them.

The Air—conductor of all sounds—seems filled
With music! In the great song of praise, which
Ever rises to the Creative Throne,
All voices seem to join, both animate
And inanimate. The tiny bird, decked
In rainbow colors, flashing from flower
To flower, from rose-buds sipping nectar,
Hums its little song; the lark rising from
Clover-fields, pours forth a flood of joyous
Music—still higher rising, back he sends
A note of wild, and fitful melody.
The bubbling fountain, babbling brook, vie with
The running stream, —with surging ocean, which
Hurls its crested wave high o'er the rocky
Ledges, and whose deep bass notes like distant
Thunder, seems as the voice of God.
    How young and fresh
Appears this Temple, built for man! God laid
The corner stone, its pillars reared, its walls
He frescoed, and its great dome He spangled
O'er with countless stars.
    Mapped out before me, lie
Snow-crowned mountains, ribboned o'er with shining

Rivulets, leaping along their rocky
Sides, as lightning leaps from a gigantic
Cloud; rich vales and fertile lands, with granite
Walls enclosed; meadows, painted in crimson,
Green and gold; luxuriant fields, teeming
With waving grain and ripening fruits. In one
Encircling ken, I gaze on rivers, lakes
And boundless oceans—on crystal glaziers,
Coral reefs, and sun-lit isles, here and there
Scattered upon her bosom, like smiling
Stars in Heaven's blue firmament. Yea, more!
I see, what seems the work of human hands;
Clustering here, are piles of marble, stone,
And brick in great variety, and most
Symmetrically arranged, all sculptured,
And nicely excavated, adapted
Well as habitations for Earth's people.
Rising in the midst, and pointing heavenward,
Are turrets, towers and domes; the streets seem
Paved, and filled with human beings, running
To and fro, crowding, jostling, dodging each
The other. How full of life, and active
Duty! each striving, doubtless, to perform

Some great and noble purpose—some holy
Work, most worthy of a soul immortal.
But scattered round, still other piles I see
Mostly of wood, in form and model like
The others—each stands alone, a garden
Plot annexed, painted in white, with training
Vines embowered, beautiful and useful;
Fit home it seems for a contented mind.
But hark! what shrill and startling sound I hear,
As of a cry of anguish—can it be
The voice of the huge monster, which I see
Dashing with lightning speed across the plains,
To the very base of rocky heights? Fire,
Steam and smoke, he belches from his nostrils.—
Madly he rushes on! now darts as does
A serpent for his hole, and disappears
Into the very bosom of the earth.
Is it the Devil? I have heard he roams
The earth, taking a serpent's form, then, that
Of angel. Lo! far beyond the rocky
Cliff, I see him dashing, flying onward
O'er shining rails, and iron-roads, scattered
Like net-work o'er earth's surface.

Lessons of Life.

How peacefully upon
The waters, move those other things of life ;
Dancing along, the towering waves they mount,
Then gently glide into the ocean's trough
Only to rise again, more proudly than
Before, scattering the spray in silvery
Showers around. Some wingless seem, others
Broad pinions have, of snowy whiteness. Can
They be male and female? All living things,
I hear are sub-divided thus ; all made
For man, for him alone created.
                Now hie me on
My mission ! and since to me permitted,
I'll take the human form,—will converse hold
With this most favored race, and from them learn
Their manners, customs, and the purposes
And aim of life, for surely, exemplars
They must be of holy living.

SCENE II.

CENTRAL PARK, NEW YORK CITY.—MORNING.

SPIRIT.

This then is Earth!
How bright and beautiful the pictured scene
Which meets my vision! rivulets. I see,
Dancing in silver light; lakelets, playing
With sunbeams; fountains, pearl drops scattering,
Forming cascades and water-falls in miniature.
Foot-paths, with evergreens embowered I see,
Winding their tortuous way, midst quiet nooks,
And rocky dells, through rich green lawns, and beds
Of flowers; forest trees, clothed with autumnal
Leaves of varied hues; these, with the structures
Man has reared, make it indeed a lovely
Spot,—almost enchanted ground.
      Here, in this
Frescade, will I sit down,—with lingering
Eye will gaze upon those laughing, joyous

Beings, now strolling round in happiness
Before me. Here comes one! bearing himself
With dignity, and on his brow enthroned,
Sits Intellect. His whitened locks, bespeak
Great wisdom and experience, while his
Pleasing eye and smiling face exhibit
Most of all, a kind and humane heart.
He, surely is the friend I seek; to him,
Will I declare myself, to him, reveal
The object of my mission, and perchance
All needed information will he give.

(He speaks to him.)

          God's peace be with thee, friend!
If looks and form belie thee not, thou wilt
Most willingly listen to a stranger's
Voice, and give him audience. Come, sit thee
Down beside me. In this pleasant spot, fanned
By the cooling breeze, together we will
Talk of God, and of his handiworks; of earth,
On which I gaze with pleasure; of man,
Respecting whom, most wondrous things abroad
Are whispered.

REV. DR. WISEMAN.

Whence, and who art thou?
Thy voice rings of the true metal, and thy
Words are indices of a mind, both pure
And virtuous.

SPIRIT.

I am no denizen of earth, but when
The great orb of day goes down, and darkness
Black as midnight gathers round, I'll point you
To a planet, which, then rising, will cast
Its borrowed light upon the world,—a soft
And pleasing light, lifting the soul heavenward,
Filling it with holy aspirations.
There is my home! 'tis in the Moon,—the great
Reflector, which at night throws sun rays on
The earth, and in turn the earth throws back
The same upon the moon. In harmony,
Each the other serves.

DR. WISEMAN.

Thou talkest nonsense, man!
Between these planets, lies immensity

Of space, crowded with sunbeams, as the sea
With rain-drops. Didst thou cross this space, as thou
Wouldst the ocean?

SPIRIT.

With God, all things are possible! Hast thou
Not heard of Angels' visits? of Spirits
In the human form, who, having done what
They were sent to do, vanished like shadows
And were seen no more?

DR. WISEMAN.

I am no Sadducee,
Who contend there is no resurrection,
Neither angel, spirit, devil; in all
I do believe, for 'tis a truth revealed
By God, and in His Holy Word proclaimed.
The soul will never die! It will exist
When the frail body crumbles into dust;
Instinct with life, 'twill burst the bonds of Earth,
And mounting up, will be enrolled among
The disembodied Spirits, be they good

Or bad. See at your feet that crawling worm!
Seemingly it will die—perhaps to-day—
If so, to-morrow it appears decked out
In rainbow colors, and on its golden
Wings, mounts upward a gaudy butterfly.
Thus the Immortal Soul, leaving at length
Its embryo state, unfettered, enters
The Spirit land, with powers well suited
For its new existence. Angels on earth
In early times appeared—angels of light,
On special missions sent, and for some wise
Purposes, while spirits satanic, were
Allowed in divers forms to roam the world,
As tempters of mankind. In latter days,
Like miracles they are not visible,
For the Great Ruler executes His vast
Designs, and purposes, by other means,
And uses other agents. Each Age, has
Had 'tis true, its own peculiar folly—
Has had its wild chimera, phantasy,
Or popular delusion, which, starting
From the brain of some half-crazed fanatic,

Has swept like wildfire, gathering in its
Course, both strength and fierceness.
                              The great hobby
Of one Age was the Crusades. The hermit
Peter, Monk of Amiens, low of stature,
And ill-favored, cŏnceived in Palestine
The grand idea of wresting from hands
Of Musselmen, our Saviour's Sepulchre,
And from infidel thralldom, rescuing
The poor Christians of the East. In his dreams,
Visions he saw, and forth he went upon
A mule, barefooted and barearmed preaching
To countless thousands. Into Italy,
And France—thence into Germany he went,
And under the banner of the Cross, millions
Were enrolled. Then, as now, enthusiasm
Was most contagious! for, seized with frenzy,
The lame, the halt and blind, with wives and children
Crowding to the Holy Land, blocked up all
Roads leading to Jerusalem. But few
Returned ! by famine, by disease, by sword,
Thousands, yea, millions fell, and Death did glut
Itself with victims.

Then came the Age
Of Witchcraft, when evil Spirits roamed
The earth, as was believed in divers forms.
Demons and Witches were plenty in those
Days;—visible, invisible, and thick
As summer flies. Aerial devils
There were, living in air, causing tempests
And whirl-winds; terrestial, dwelling on earth,
The timid frightening, and tormenting men.
Witchcraft became a mania. Foolish,
And absurd, this vile belief engendered
Superstitions, which in their turn deluged
The land with blood—with horrors, too terrible
To relate. Learned and unlearned, old and young,
The beautiful maiden and the toothless
Hag, were all bewitched, and on the scaffold,
Or at the stake they suffered. Was there time,
I could relate of other ages most
Strange delusions; how thorough search was made
For the *Elixir Vitae*,—thought to be
Of death a sure preventative; of search
For the Philosopher's Stone, which, if found
Would turn all metals into gold, making

Men rich; of Divination, Augury,
Magnetism and Prophecy, till coming
Down, a tale I could relate, of midnight
Seances, moonlight materializations,
And of dark circles, wherein spirits, white
And black appear, exhibiting most strange
And marvelous manifestations.
                                Mysterious
Is that influence, by which one mind can
Sway another, as the will doth ever
Sway the members of the body, making
Them do its bidding; more mysterious,
The seeming willingness exhibited
By some, in being blindly led, against
Their judgment, reason, conscience, and against
All common sense, into glaring errors,
Adopting theories, and principles
Pernicious in themselves, absurd, and most
Destructive to society. God made
The mind as He made stars, perfect! and as
In Nature's diadem He set those brilliants,
So in the world of intellect.—His own
Bright coronet—did He fix the mind, and gave

It strength His glory to reflect, as moon
Throws back the sun-rays. How sad to know that
This, the noblest portion of our being,
Which thinks, and wills, and reasons,—this gifted
Reflex of the Deity, should comet-like
Have broken from its sphere, o'er leaping bounds
Fixed by the Almighty, and gone rambling
Through space, casting but shadows. Ofttimes
At night, while gazing on the stars twinkling
So beautifully in the heavens, have
I seen a meteor go flashing through
The sky, earthward, then in black darkness
Disappear. Thus man did fall from the high
Estate in which he was created.

SPIRIT.

Indeed! most marvelous
Things thou dost relate, of thine own species.
In yonder planet, peopled by a race
Guiltless and sinless, something was whispered
Of the fall of man, and of some special favor,
Wherein was exercised an attribute
Of Deity never before displayed,—
Of mercy and forgiveness. More would we

Learn, and to this end it was permitted
Me to visit earth, and in human form
To sojourn for a while. Ambassador,
Unheralded, and unannounced I come
Upon this special mission! no regal
Pomp, no brilliant retinue attend my
Footsteps; no boon companion will lend his
Aid and presence, nor with me, share the work
And honor of this my high vocation.
Alone, I'll range through earth, observing man
In public, social, and in private life ;
Will note his actions, read his thoughts, and trace
The inward workings of his mind. Thy words
Cast shadows o'er my spirits, and drink up
Pleasant thoughts, as darkness drinks up twilight.
Surely 'mong God's favored ones, can be found
A host of noble, just, and virtuous
Men, whose every word, and thought, and act, must
Harmonize with the Creative Mind?

>> DR. WISEMAN.
I would not take
One virtue from the human heart, nor add
One pang to thine; but if indeed thou art

A Spirit as thou dost say, and here have
Come upon a holy mission, God speed
Thy footsteps, and give thee strength thy duty
To perform. Deceitful above all things,
And desperately wicked, is the heart
Uncleansed and unredeemed. Go the world o'er,
From Frost Land to the Burning Zone, from East
To West, 'mong Christians, Pagans, civilized
And uncivilized, and you will see dark
Crimes committed, foul wrongs perpetrated,
And fiery passions like fiends incarnate,
Each striving for the mastery. Enough
You'll see to give thee heart-throbs, driving
The blood, hot, tingling through the veins.

    Among the masses of mankind,
There have in every age been found good men,
Whose characters like burnished gold, have shone
Spotless and pure. Generous, unselfish,
Full of faith and holy love, they have lived
Not for themselves, but to promote the good
Of others, and magnify the great name
Of Him who governs all. Like Oases
In a barren desert, so in the moral

Lessons of Life.

World, where everything seems scorched, and
   shriveled
Up by sin, such characters look fruitful
And most refreshing. Unknown, unhonored
They may be—on history's page their names
May be unwritten; it matters not! for in
The great Book of Life they are enrolled.
                    Wouldst thou learn
The story of our Race—its progress trace
From the creation to the present time,
Or know the human mind, and understand
Its varied changes, from early infancy
To age advanced—from cradle to the grave?
On history's page, sacred and profane
'Tis written; the records of all ages ·
Therein are treasured up; God's dealings with
Our race, and all essential facts are there
Spread out, like stars upon the firmament

SPIRIT.

             How happens it,
That for so many years these facts could be
Remembered—the records how preserved?

DR. WISEMAN.

The mind is ever active, either
For good or evil. Now doth it wander,
In day-dreams, fictions, and visions from place
To place, by truth or reason unrestrained,—
Then, will it gather facts, search out events,
And by comparison, will discover
The external relations they bear, each
To the other. Most complex is the mind's
Phenomena, for mingling together
Like the ingredients of a compound,
Are thoughts, sensations, and emotions, each
Striving for the mastery, giving new
Life and force to mental faculties. On
Science, all Arts practical, are founded;
And what is science but the glorious
Product of the mind, in comprehending
The relationship of things, and tracing
Effects back to their causes? Truly,
This Age is an inventive one! In art,
And science, most rapid progress has been
Made, and marvelous things revealed during

The present century. The printing press
By steam is driven, and books, a countless
Number are scattered o'er the world. In Greek,
Hebrew, Syraic, Arabic,—in French,
German, English,—in poetry, and prose
Are now recorded the past and present
Of our race.
    In his great wisdom, God hath to us
Revealed His Holy Will,—instructed us
In matters pertaining to Himself, His
Government, and of the grand scheme by Him
Devised for man's redemption. Of all books,
Most precious is the Bible! It recounts
The history of man from the creation
. To the present time; the simple story
Of the cross it tells—how God this guilty
World so loved, as to give His only Son
A sacrifice for sin, how willingly
The Son did drink the bitter cup, thereby
Perfecting man's redemption.
    Yea, more! this blessed book,
Filled with most glorious truths, and precious
Promises,—with holy precepts and sweet

Messages of love, shines like a beacon
Light, to guide the wandering soul into
The haven of Eternal Rest.

SPIRIT.

And is this true?
Such love I cannot comprehend! Why did
Not God blast this sinful world, or make it
Pure by his avenging lightnings?

DR. WISEMAN.

God is Love! and being such,
He freely did forgive, and gave His Son
A ransom for our race. All can be saved
Who will repent in faith.—Not otherwise.

SPIRIT.

Did you say, that rapid progress now
Was being made, in science and in art?

DR. WISEMAN.

Like Ocean's crested waves,
Years onward rush in the great sea of Time,
Bringing to light the products of man's skill

And ingenuity. How quick years come
And go, then vanish into ages, crowned
With events and monuments stupendous!
Time was, when the frail body was enslaved
And doomed to servile labor. The daily
Bread by the brow's sweat was earned, and toiling
Millions had no higher aim, or purpose,
Than to get food and raiment. How little
Did they know of mind, its giant powers,
And God-like faculties! For long ages
It slept in fetters—barren and sterile
As deserts' burning sands, but rousing up,
At length it burst its bonds, and to the world
Proclaimed its high prerogatives. Time works
Its changes, and for two centuries past,
Mind has been active, and the world has moved.
Most rapid and universal is social
Intercourse; with lightning speed oceans are
Traversed, deserts explored, and now being
Fully developed is the philosophy
Of uses. Most rapid strides have nations
Made in science and in art—wind, water,
Fire are harnessed up to do man's bidding,

And night and day they toil, driving those huge
Machines, which now perform man's servile work.

                    But see! the evening cometh—
The lengthening shadows and descending sun
Bid us depart. Come to my home and see
Domestic life. Before the Throne of Grace,
With us unite in prayer and praise to Him,
Who doth all things well.

SCENE III.

WALL STREET.—NOON.

SPIRIT.

Strange sight is this!
What means this human tide, this hurrying
To and fro, this crowding, jostling, dodging
Each the other? Feverish, excited
They appear, but full of life and action
Vigorous. Surely, some great and noble
Purpose they must have, some worthy object;
Competitors perhaps, for the great prize,—
The Crown of Glory, God has offered.

DR. WISEMAN.

In his dark cell,
A felon, convicted and condemned, will
Sometimes fall asleep, and a sweet, joyous
Smile will play upon his countenance, while
He dreams of home, of happy, boyhood days,
And of a mother's love. I would not,—could

Not have the heart this dream-sketch to despoil,
Or from his mind drive out this vision bright,
For soon enough he'll wake to misery.
Nor would I, were it not expedient,
Wake you from day-dreams, or blur this vision
Of your soul as to our race. 'Tis Mammon
Worship you behold! here sits the golden
Calf enthroned, and at its most exacting
Shrine, men offer incense. To rob, and cheat
Seems their chief end,—their sought for *summum bonum*.

The savage in his pride, points to the scalps
Suspended from his person, as trophies
Of his power; the purse-proud millionaire
Exhibits gold, wrung from the poor man's brow,
And calls it wealth; yea! the jeweled upstart,
Who deals in stocks, and bonds, and money loans
At most usurious rates, will rack his brain
To take the bread from out his brother's mouth.
Go in the " Broker's Board," or the " Exchange,"
And you will see how men like cats and dogs
Will snarl and growl, one at the other. We
Call them " *Bulls and Bears*,"—fit names for those

Lessons of Life.   129

Who prey upon each other. Thirsting for
Gold, how demon-like they act, and what vile
Tricks they practice, to deceive and cheat their
Fellows. 'Tis a School of Vice, wherein base
Passions rule, and legalized is gambling.
     Here dissemblers meet, and here
Do congregate a class of men, who pit
Their brains against their hearts, and having left
At home their consciences, will bring their bags
Of yellow gold, and with them practice most
Infernal arts. Here too, are seen the young
And inexperienced. Led on by dazzling
Dreams of wealth, and hopes delusive, they will
Step by step, this whirlpool of corruption
Enter, till they are fleeced and robbed of all
Their honest earnings. Not content with this
Deserved chastisement, manhood they barter,
And their honor pledge as one would pawn
His jewels, at most usurious rates.
Cheating one's self is bad enough, but when
'Tis done, how easy to practice the same
Game on others. By fraud, some men grow rich
And others poor. This gambling legalized,

Petrifies the soul,—hath drank all goodness
From the heart, as death will drink its life-blood.
Well hath the poet said—
" In the street the tide of being, how it surges, how
    it rolls—
God! what base ignoble faces. God! what bodies
    wanting souls."

SPIRIT.

    Thy words indeed are terrible!
Like drops of molten lead, into my heart
They burn. Why does not God hurl forth his bolts,
And blast them with his vengeance? why bestow
On such as these, his gifts of love, or strew
With flowers their pathway—scattering blessings.
On them like snow-flakes o'er the earth? Is gold
Man's only idol, and this the only
Plague spot of the world, or at other shrines,
And in other lands is incense offered?

DR. WISEMAN.

    Man's folly is proverbial!
How full of human blunders, ignorance,
And crime is the historic page! It tells

Of mad ambition, grasping avarice,
And venal lust, of selfishness most base,
Of tyranny most horrible. These are
The idols, men everywhere do worship.
Man delights in power, and when obtained
How wrongfully he uses it! The vile
Pestilence which stalketh forth at noonday,
Dragging its countless victims in its train,
Is less destructive than the tyrant's will.
Let elements combine, let all unite
With the destroying angel in blotting
God's image from the earth—yea! the Sea
May lash herself to fury, volcanic
Fires may rage, earthquakes may rock earth's centre,
The fierce tornado hither and thither,
Dash, wildly insane,—'tis all in vain!
Elements their rest must take from such mad
Efforts, and human wisdom will foresee,
And guard against destruction.
     Not so with human passions!
For once inflamed, like fires of Hell, they burn,
And burn forever. Tyrants are fiends
In human form,—incarnate fiends! who prey

Upon mankind, and glut themselves with blood.
Man's bitter foe, is man, and they will feed
Like carrion crows upon each other.
> This Age
Is noted for its crimes, among those deemed
Respectable. Scarcely a day doth pass,
Without its breathing some gigantic fraud,
Or startling defalcation,—not by the poor,
And so-called vulgar class committed,
But by those honored wretches who have lived
In princely style, dazzling our eyes by means
Of borrowed wealth,—perhaps by those whom we
To power have raised, custodians made
Of our great nation's treasures. Alas; 'tis true!
The very air seems surcharged as with crime,
The winds do whisper in our ears some truths,
Which cause our hearts to throb, our cheeks with
>> blood
To crimson, and our eyes, hot, scalding tears
To drop for very shame. How true as one
Has said, "It matters not what men assume
To be, or good, or bad, they are but what
They are."

Lessons of Life.

To rob, and cheat, and steal,
Is a prerogative assumed by some,
Who seek thereby to magnify themselves,
And lord it over others. With costly
Wines and sumptuous dinners, they attach
A class of hungry sycophants, who dog-like
Fawn upon their tinseled masters,—ready
Stand to do their bidding, and to their every
Word will say, Amen! How rocket-like some
Men with rushing sound, will rise above their
Fellows, and to the gaping crowd throw off
Most brilliant scintillations,—for a time
In dazzling brightness they are seen, then all
Is darkness; yea! like a charred stick they fall,—
Are trampled on, by once admiring friends.
Don't call this luck, or chance—No! No! but God,
Whose great Omniscient eye beholdeth all
Things, and Who the secrets of the inmost heart
Doth read, may for a little while permit
Such fools to glory in their shame, before
He hurls them to destruction.
     I know one,
And with his case we are all familiar,

Who, but yesterday was the "Grand Mogul"
Of a powerful faction. Stalwart in frame,
And schooled in politics, the central figure
Was he in a Ring most infamous. He
Was its Chief, its head, its front, and as such
Was he worshipped. Daring, unscrupulous,
A crafty trickster, and designing knave,
He had an eye on plunder. Ambition
Was the spur of all his actions ;—the God
To which he sacrificed—what most he should
Have guarded,—his honor and his manhood.
In his enormous grasp, he seized what came
Within his reach,—no matter whence it came,
Or how; it was his gold and wealth. The man,
Who in public, or official duty
Fails, on private virtue will disdainful
Tread, as steps to raise him to some higher
Purpose. Rogues who dread shame, to hide their
    guilt
Will greater rogues become. Guilt once begun,
Will fly to crime consummate to be safe.
Rich and powerful had become this crafty
Politician; then followed in his train

A crowd of fawning sycophants, to whom
His smile was life, and death his frown. Judges
Were but his tools, and Legislators classed
Among his warmest friends ; Courts he controlled
And ballot box he stuffed ; Schools political,
In which the vile and ignorant of earth
Were gathered, to be trained his will to do,
Were lavishly supported.
     Oh! how like
Summer insects, did these parasites bask
Awhile in sunshine, and with gilded wings,
Flutter about this tinseled lord. How fat
And sleek they grew on stolen provender,
Scattered so lavishly by the Boss's hand ;
How every man at will did grind his axe,—
And axes were plenty in those days—each,
And all, some grinding needed on " My Lord's"
Great model grindstone,—" Corruption." In his
Pride the Chief grew most presumptuous! had he
Lived on buttered thunder, and drank naught else
But vivid lightnings, more gorgeous villainies
He could not have displayed, to shock mankind.
Oh! how he piled up wrath, against the day

Of wrath,—his power supreme, he would snap
His fingers in faces of honest men,
And threaten them with vengeance.

SPIRIT.

Didst thou not say but yesterday,
That brutes by instinct know their foes, and when
To them superior strength is given,
They use it for destruction? Didst thou not
Say the veriest worm when trampled on.
Turns on its destroyer? Why then do men
Endowed with reason—with powers of thought
And action,—with determined will, tamely
Submit to such ignoble acts? why not
Crush out at once such human monsters?

DR. WISEMAN.

This man had sown the wind,
And now the whirlwind of the people's wrath
Must surely reap. Such potent instruments
By them had been prepared, as would o'erturn
This Idol of the hour, and dash him down
By proofs invincible. The Ring of which
He was the head and front, was broken up,
And craven minions by guilty conscience

Lessons of Life. 137

Lashed, like chaff before the wind were scattered.
Thank God! the time had come when could be found
A Jury who dared convict,—an honest
Judge, who dared the penalty due to crime
Inflict; whom bribes did not affect, and who
Firmly and justly the law administered.
The great man was arrested, and his day
Of glory set in darkest night. Justice
This once had triumphed. Cold, pale and trembling,
This helpless, shipwrecked wretch was made to stand
In public; with uncovered head received
The sentence of the Court,—not death, but deep,
Damning degradation. Honors and wealth,
The intercourse with friends, comforts of home,
Yea! the world itself must be abandoned,
And thus for twelve long years, with shaven head,
Wearing the garb of infamy and shame,
Must he live and toil with convicts. Punishment
Deserved! How thick the thoughts did crowd upon
His wearied brain,—scorpion-like, each one
Did have its sting; the Future, Present, Past;

Oh! how like molten lead they fell upon
His smitten soul to weigh it down. By night,
By day did guilty conscience like a fiend
Torment him, and if perchance, upon his
Hard, cold cot he fell asleep, of nightmare
'Twould take the form, and scare him till the flesh
Seemed creeping from the bone and he woke up
In misery.
The galley-slave while tugging at the oar,
Can feel no degradation if ignoble
Born; but he, who in the lap of luxury
Is bred, whose every wish is gratified,
Whose word is law, endowed with mental powers
And with a mind most richly cultivated,—
A millionaire, ranking among the noble
Ones of earth, Oh! he will feel like sinking
Out of sight, his bonds will hang like mill-stones
Round his neck to sink him to perdition.

SPIRIT

'Tis a burning shame!
That men will train the passions, the vices
Cultivate, will gloss misdeeds, and trifle
With great truths. This love of power,—this lust

For gold must prostitute the soul, and make
'It ripe for infamy.

     DR. WISEMAN.

      Alas! tis true;
Like mildew, it will blast and shrivel up
The good within us. The sordid Judas
Did for paltry gold betray his Lord,
And to the rabble, thirsting for His blood,
The ambitious Pilate gave his Master.
Enough of this.—Let us go hence.

SCENE IV.

BROADWAY.—AFTERNOON.

SPIRIT.

Here do I breathe more freely.
From my soul has passed a frightful vision,
Like vapor from the earth. I seem to stand
In sunlight, and the night-shadows of my
Spirit, before the glory and grandeur
Of this enchanted spot, have vanished.
How young, and fresh, and beautiful appear
The objects of my vision! These marble
Palaces, these marts of trade with crystal
Fronts, filled with earth's choicest products; these
    domes
And spires ascending heavenward; these laughing,
Joyous faces,—lovely maidens, in form
Angelic, and whose smiles, sweet as opening
Rose-buds are showered upon us,—surely,
These are true indices of a mind, pure,
Happy and contented.

DR. WISEMAN.

Like oxen yoked together,
Science and Art their forces have combined,
To beautify the world's great promenades.
For miles extends this broad, paved thoroughfare,
Lined with continuous freestone, granite and
Marble, chiseled, sculptured and embellished
With costly decorations, symmetrical
And elaborate. Here too, ebbs and flows
Unceasingly, the great tide of human
Life. bearing upon its spacious bosom,
People of every nation, clime, and tongue.
Here side by side, are starving mendicants
And purse-proud millionaires; the virtuous
Maidens and painted courtesans; the man
Of thought and action, and the brainless fop.
Here, Votaries of Fashion you can see,
Swarming these trade-temples, like bees about
A hive, buzzing from store to store, feasting
Their eyes on newest styles, and most recent
Importations. Maidens, matrons, mothers
In dressy toilets, vie with flaunting belles,
In gathering tinseled gewgaws to bedeck

Their persons. Shopping, is but a habit,
Most dangerous and expensive. It has
Made kind husbands bankrupt,—to untimely
Graves sent parents broken-hearted,—cheapened
Virtue, and made the young both proud and vain,
By dressing them like puppets for a show.
          " Going-a-shopping,"
Is a phrase by the many used—by few
Well understood. Not simply does it mean
Comforts and necessities to purchase;
O, no!—It means to promenade the streets
In gorgeous suits, or toilets elegant,—
Seeing and being seen,—flirting with those
With whom they come in contact, yea! flirting
With nice young men who ready stand to show
Them due attention. It means absenting
One's self from home, leaving the "little ones,"
Perhaps an infant babe,—from morn till night
To tender mercies of a cruel nurse;—
It means keeping one's self from "rusting out,"—
Life's precious moments wasting in a whirl
Continuous, of giddy dissipation.

SPIRIT.

Speak not I pray thee, so bitterly
Of woman! whom God hath made beautiful
As Venus,—pure and bright as morning star.
Surely, there are those whose lives of spotless
Purity, like virgin gold are modest,
And of intrinsic value.

DR. WISEMAN.

Thou speakest truly!
At the creation, the great and crowning
Work of God was woman—man's helpmate
And companion. Most beautiful, most frail
Was she created, and when tempted—fell;
Man also fell, and evil filled the world
As brine doth fill the ocean. Redemption
Came!—Seed of the woman bruised the serpent's
Head. The Virgin Mother bore a cherub
Boy; "Immanuel," He was called,—the "Prince
Of Peace,"—the "Saviour" of the world. Angels
Might well rejoice, and Stars together sing,
When in a humble manger Christ appeared,
Born of a woman. Honored and redeemed
She stands, exalted above all others.

Yes! thousands there are
In this great mammon city, whose home-life
Seems as sweet and cheerful as the placid
Lake, shut in twixt mountainets. Woman's
True empire is her home, and power she
Hath, by influence and by example,
To make, or mar domestic life. Modest,
Cheerful, amiable, she wins her crown
Of glory by noble acts, and being
What she is, the crown and blessing of her
Family. "What so beautiful on earth,
As kindred love and family repose?
Home is a world in minature, with Sun
And Moon, and galaxy of shining Stars,
Moving in love and harmony. Filial
Obedience and parental care go hand
In hand, like two young loves, seeking each
Others' happiness   Here the fond mother
Does her noblest work; in faith and joyous
Hope, in prayers and tears, with constant care
And deep solicitude, the characters
Of her little ones she forms and daily
Moulds, watering, and pruning these olive

Plants, 'round the parental board." Thus does she
Gild a virtuous life, with brighest gold.

SPIRIT.

Thou showest me now,
Summer and sunshine of domestic life,
And should I here on earth remain, methinks
'Mong the fair daughters of the land, a wife
I would select,—no tinseled fashionist ;
No made-up manakin, or flirting belle,
But one possessing reason, conscience, heart ;
Whose gentle manners, and whose modest ways
Like Autumn clouds upon the evening sky,
Scatter their roseate hues of beauty
And of love on all around.   Pray tell me
Sir, do all men marry?

DR. WISEMAN.

O, no! for some there are,
Whose hearts are cold as snow-drifts, sterile as
Icelandic icebergs, who can no more love
Than marble statue, chiseled to human
Form.   Selfish, phlegmatic, onward through life
They grope their way, unloving and unloved.

Others there are,
Habitues of gilded sample-rooms, oft
Seen at places like the Cremorne, Mabille,
And Bagnios—the fast young men, whose lives
Are sensual, and wretched made by vice,
And lowest dissipation; such prefer
A mistress to a wife; a club or dance
House, to a quiet fireside. Thus they grow
Old in sin, and make a boast of single
Blessedness.

SPIRIT.

Rather say
They glory in their shame! for shameless must
They be, who to unbridled passions give
The greatest latitude. It seems most strange,
That the immortal mind can thus debase
Its mortal tenement,—can blast the spring-buds
Of its life, as the young plant is blasted
By the early frost. Surely, with a cold
Eye the world must frown upon them, and from
Its presence drive these wretched sensualists.

DR. WISEMAN.

Not so! In the great
Play-house of the world, either in Comedy,

Or Tragedy, all take a part and each
A chacter assumes, conspicuous
Or humble. Before the blazing foot-lights,
Folly and Fortune hand in hand appear,—
Stars of the first magnitude in worldling's
Eyes, who laud them to the skies and on them
Shower repeated encores. Next Wisdom
And Virtue—the twin-sisters come, bearing
Themselves with grace and modesty; admired
Indeed by few, but by the great masses
Scorned and derided. Great is the power
Of Wealth! like charity it covereth
A multitude of sins. The sensualist,
However vile a vagabond, is dined
And wined; is petted, toadied and caressed
Provided he is rich. His wealth doth gild
His character, as the dark angry cloud
Ofttimes is gilded 'round with burnished
Sun-rays. Gold gives position, sanctifies
All vice, and into crystal lakes transforms
These cesspools of corruption. 'Tis lunch time!
Our bodies frail, food, drink and rest require.

As the parched earth refreshing showers. Wilt
Go with me?

SPIRIT.

Most willingly do I accept
Your hospitalities. Let us depart.

SCENE V.

FIFTH AVENUE.—MORNING.

DR. WISEMAN.

These are the abodes of men
Who live in style, and roll in luxury.
These stately, brown stone mansions, towering
Skyward, ornate, elaborate, for miles
Extend, and to the eye seem palaces
In dream-land. Within these massive walls, fresh
From the hands of artists and artizans,
Are brilliant frescoes, and most beautiful
Decorations. Here Parian busts are seen
On golden tripods, and the costliest,
Rarest statuary from pure marble
Sculptured, stand singly or in groups. Alcoves,
With crimson velvet hung; carpets of gobelin,
Soft and luxuriant; tables, inlaid
With ivory and with pearl, bronzes, vases,
And matchless paintings, are all reflected
In the huge, polished mirrors, and combine

With the Parisian furniture to form
A picture of gorgeous magnificence.
Here Princes dwell, and here they exercise
A glorious exclusiveness. From these
Palatial homes, with scorn they look upon
The honest laborer, who toils to earn
His daily bread. The stately oak, towering
Above its fellows will bask in sunshine,
And will toy with sunbeams playing among
Its branches; but no fruit it bears, except
The stinted acorn, while on the fruitful
Trees it looks with cold contempt, and o'er them
Throws its darkened shadow. Thus with these men,
Living a life of quietude and ease,
Basking in sunlight of prosperity,
Selfish, arrogant and proud, what care they
For starving millions, or less fortunate
Ones of earth, to whom they lend no helping
Hand, but on them cast the cold, dark shadow
Of contempt.

SPIRIT.

Thou dost call them Princes;
Are they descendants of a nobler race,

Or made of nobler blood than others? In
Intellect, or powers of mind, do they
Excel?

DR. WISEMAN.

Appearances are
Most deceitful. The tawdry sunflower,
Upon its high and branchless stalk, will turn
Itself in pride, keeping its yellow disk
Looking sunward while in its shadow grows
The modest violet, or fragrant rose,
Most rare and beautiful. The noblest ones
Of earth, live not in gilded palaces,
Nor stand they high in the great world's opinion.
'Tis on earth's surface barren rocks are seen,
And bleak cold mountains lie—in her bosom,
Silver and gold, and purest ores and gems
Of priceless value lie concealed. These men
Are shoddy princes! from obscurity
They sprung, like mushrooms from a dung hill. Here
Comes one! his paneled carriage drawn by well
Groomed horses, driven by liveried servants.
How like a Lord he seems,—looking at what
He is—not what he was. Can you believe,

His father was but a common huckster,
And his mother a vender of apples
In the market? Such they were,—a thrifty
Couple on whom Dame Fortune smiled, and they
Secured a competence. This son, crafty,
Shrewd, unprincipled, grew up to manhood,
Leading a shameful life of idleness,
And dissipation. Somehow, or other—
Rumor doth not tell—he floated into
Politics; a wire-puller soon became,
Leader of caucuses—of cliques and rings;
A power behind the throne, obtaining
For himself and friends, offices yielding
Perquisites immense, and rich, fat contracts—
Those stupendous frauds—whereby the city
Was defrauded, and he enriched.
This self-made man—and that he made himself
There is no doubt—is now a millionaire,
Drives daily to his club, idling his time
Away with men, as honest as himself.

SPIRIT.

Have they no noble purpose—
No great end in view? Powerful and rich,

How easily could they strew with flowers
The pathway of the poor, pluck thorns from hearts
Most deeply lacerated—comfort give
To widows and the fatherless.

DR. WISEMAN.

Thou speakest nonsense!
Their souls are bound, as the Chinese do bind
Their feet to make them small, and when old age
Comes on, the heart all dried and shriveled up,
Is but a lump of selfishness—a piece
Of petrifaction, harder than adamant.
Searching, scrambling for wealth is the great aim
Of life, and miser-like they'll hug their gold,
Even when tottering o'er their graves, and death
Films make them sightless. Not of all I speak!
For there are those—exceptions to the rule—
Who at the Judgment-Seat, will hear the words,
"Well done thou good and faithful servant."

SPIRIT.

Have these most selfish men, no fear of death,
Or the great future spreading out before
Them, like a vast, trackless ocean?

DR. WISEMAN.

    Yes! as the mariner dreads
The typhoon, so they dread death—they hate it,
As nature hates a vacuum. Feeling
Within themselves a consciousness of life
Immortal, they grasp it, as a drowning
Man a straw, foolishly applying it,—
Not to the soul, but to its frail, earthy
Tenement. To them, the thought of endless
Life—of infinite eternity *on earth*,
Is most delightful.—Oh! how they bask
In sunshine, boasting of wealth and power;
Hoarding their riches as the miser does
His gold, and for a little time rehearse
The parody on life—then beggar-like
They die, and but a tomb stone tells the spot
Where lie their fleshless bones; soon into dust
Even this marble crumbles, and by howling
Winds is swept away. Friends mourn a single
Day, clothing themselves in sackcloth, and o'er
Their graves will drop a tear, then like a pack
Of hounds, will fight and squabble for a share
Of the estate.

Lessons of Life.

Grim Death to all will come!
Surely as the Winter's frosts, or Summer's
Heat. The little cherub boy, with head all
Covered o'er with clustering ringlets; with cheeks
Crimsoned with purest life-blood; reclining
On his mother's lap, his simple prayer
Will lisp—then with a good night kiss will fall
Sweetly asleep, dreaming of bright angels
Even while Death, taking the form of croup,
Noiselessly, stealthily appears and robs
The lovely casket of its bright, jeweled
Spirit. The full-grown man, most perfectly
Developed, muscular and sinewy,
May boast his health and strength, but ere the words
Have fallen from his lips, Death in the form
Of apoplexy strikes him dead. The King
Upon his throne must die, as in the street
The beggar. As naked born, so naked
Must we go from earth and be forgotten.
Death is a leveler! No wise distinctions
Doth he make of caste, or color. Mankind
He serves alike, and if on one he fixes
His cold eye, that man will die, let him be

Prince or beggar. For all, he hath prepared
A common bed, and side by side, he lays
The rich man with the poor—master with slave,
And o'er them throws the same cold, earthy
Mantle.
    O, Death! thou art insatiable!
Thou dost come in war, in peace, in earthquakes,
Lightnings, storms; in pestilential vapors,
And cooling zephyrs. Merciless, bribeless,
Pitiless—a dreaded vampire, thou dost
Glut thyself with victims, and still remain
Unsatisfied.

SPIRIT.

    Thou speakest truly, but thy words
Are full of sadness, weighing most heavily
On my spirit. But see! gathered before
Us, a thronging multitude; canst thou tell
Its meaning?

DR. WISEMAN.

    In yonder spacious mansion lies
A human form, lifeless and cold. The heart
Throbs not, and the pulse has ceased its faintest
Beating. Within the veins and arteries,

No life-blood flows, for like the rivulets
Of Spring drank up by the parched summer's earth,
So it has vanished; while the brain wearied,
And faint, has given up unfinished, its
Life-engrossing business. The man is dead!
Within a gorgeous casket, embowered
In loveliest flowers, lie the remains
Of the so-called—" Merchant Prince." He has gone
Naked and alone, into the Spirit
Land, leaving behind his vast estates, his
Goods, chattels, lands, stocks, bonds; his gold and all
That could be gathered up in that short space
Of time—that moment we call–" Life." How strange!
That men will toil—and rack the brain, and strain
Their heart-strings, for no nobler purpose than
To gather up the dross of earth. The dead
To earth must be consigned, and friends have met
Together, to perform the last, sad rite
Of burial—a duty, the living
Owe the dead. Let us depart.

SCENE VI.

THE BATTERY.—EVENING.

SPIRIT.

      In every form God seems to bless
Mankind, and watches them as tenderly,
As a young mother does her first-born babe.
To-night I feel His presence, for I see
All scattered round about us, His handi-
Works—expressions of His love, and warmest
Sympathy. The moon shines in her glory,
And smooth as glass, the waters of the bay,
Unrippled by the cooling breeze wafted
From the great sea beyond. The countless stars,
Like eyes of Cherubim and Seraphim,
Seem smiling on us, while nature, all clothed
In queenly majesty, whispers to our
Souls the words of peace and comfort.

DR. WISEMAN.

      Thou speakest truly! The sun,
The moon, the countless stars; with system piled

On system, and far beyond, other suns,
And other systems—each in its order,
Like clock-work moving—are but exhibits
Of the handiwork of the Great Infinite,
Whose love, boundless as space and durable
As eternity, we all experience.
     On us, and on our race
He scatters blessings, like pearly dew-drops
On the parched earth, for 'tis in Him we
Live, and move, and have our being. God clothes,
And feeds the lily of the field—teaches
The sparrow how to build its nest, and rear
Its young, and to everything created,
Animal, and vegetable, He gives
The most exquisite structure, and complete
Organization. On all space we see
God's footprints, and every mind bears imprint
Of His Divinity.
     'Tis a lovely night!
Bright and beautiful every thing appears,
Viewed from this quiet spot. Behind us lies
This giant city, seemingly at rest,
But full of life,—active and restless.

SPIRIT.

Why do men labor thus?
Must they ever toil—straining their sinews,
And racking the brain, simply to obtain
Earth's comforts and necessities?

DR. WISEMAN.

On promises, or sympathizing words,
Men cannot live. 'Tis true, the arid rock
To the dry moss yields nutriment, but men,
Machine-made slaves, must toil, and sweat, and trudge,
From early dawn, to night's dark hours, simply
To wring from stony hearts of their tyrant
Masters, life's bare necessities! Many such there are and ever
Will be, so long as man's inhumanity
To man continues; not of these I speak,
But of the masses seen in our crowded
Thoroughfares, and theatres—in the haunts
Of vice, and dens of infamy. 'Tis a wild,
Thoughtless age, of gaming and extravagance.
Men blaspheme God! they worship sordid gold,

Which makes them selfish, arrogant and bold;
Gold gives position, sanctifies all vice,
Freezes the life-blood, turns the heart to ice;
Our shoddy princes, neither toil, nor till,
But spring like mushrooms, from the foul dunghill.

SPIRIT.

Men blaspheme God! Surely, it cannot be!
Methinks the avenging Angel would have
Struck them dead!

DR. WISEMAN.

God's ways, are not as our ways,
Nor His thoughts, as the thoughts of man. He strikes
Not dead at once the ruthless villain, who,
In cold blood, murders the sinless infant,
Or who robs the widow, and fatherless
Of their rights. Deceitful above all things,
Is the human heart, and desperately
Wicked, but of this thou knowest little.
The ministerial robe should not be worn,
To cover leprous rags of sin-polluted
Wretch, or 'neath its folds, conceal a moral

Vagabond, though he can boast a giant's
Intellect. Mind was created for high
And noble purposes, but when depraved,
'Twill mask itself ofttimes in godliness,
And preach most holy truths, with sin-polluted
Lips. Men boast their love of country, but proud,
Ambitious, full of self-conceit, will act
As foolish, as did the Eastern King, who,
Flushed with ambitious pride, proposed to strike
The head from Jupiter's Statue, and place
His own thereon.—Others will traitors prove ;
For gold, will sell their country—their birthright,
For a mess of pottage.

    Some thrive as villains thrive—by deeds
So horrible as to startle nature,
And alarm the world. Pride, envy, malice,
Hate, engender stormy passions—make men
Ambitious, rash and insolent. The man,
Who casts aside, all duty and allegiance,
Distorting truth, and trampling on all law—
Who shackles reason, and spurns the whisperings
Of his conscience, is a dangerous traitor,
Wedded to his shame ; ever should he be

A mark of scorn, the world's derision; while
The stings of conscience, and bitter curses
Of mankind, should make life hateful to him.
    'Twas but last evening,
In spacious hall, crowded with old and young,
The thoughtless and the gay, a learned man,
Ranking high among his fellows; with gifts
Rich and exhaustless; with eloquence bold
And persuasive, and with an oily tongue,
Did willfully declare—"there is no God!
No Judgment! no Immortal Life!" Boldly,
He scoffed at sacred things—blasphemed the name
Of the Almighty, and in sarcastic,
And defiant tones, cast base ridicule,
And low contempt on God's most Holy Word.
    Like some destroying plague,
Which carries in its train both misery
And death, so were his words most contagious,
And poisonous to the vast crowd before
Him, who by applause and encores oft made,
Manifested their approval. O Shame!
Shame!—God might then have hurled a thunder-
 bolt,

And struck them dead, or the arm have palsied
And tongue have withered, of this rash and bold
Blasphemer.   Not so however! sunlight
Still, He throws athwart his pathway, gives him
Health and strength, feeds and clothes his little ones,
And blessings without number showers upon
Him.   Thus, He may continue, permitting
This most ungrateful wretch, to pile up wrath
Against the day of wrath.

SPIRIT.

'Tis terrible to contemplate!
This vile scoffer of sacred things, whose breath
Is in his nostrils, and who with scornful
Steps, doth tread the path of life—standing with
Duty and with Deity, in reckless,
Bold defiance, must surely know that God
Exists, and feel within himself Immortal
Life.   Can he honestly doubt it?

DR. WISEMAN.

God made the mind
To think, and will, and reason—on it stamped

Some *Great First Truths*, foundation of all our
Reasoning. Is it not true, that every
Event must have a cause—one adequate
To the effect? and in vast Nature's works,
Should we not infer the intelligence,
The powers and attributes of the *First
Great Cause?* By laws fixed and uniform, all
Natural things are governed. There, out upon
The water, onward so swiftly gliding,
Is a Steamship driven by machinery
Most complicated—made, and designed by
Man. See its changing course! moving hither
And thither, 'mong the great fleet of anchored
Vessels, and without colliding, passes ·
Them. At the helm, a pilot stands, skilful
And intelligent—his will and judgment
Directs her course.
    Thus, was perfected and designed,
The more complicated machinery
Of the universe; planets and systems
Put in motion, and guided in their course,
By a mind designing, and intelligent—
One infinite in wisdom, boundless in

Power—self-existent and eternal.
In the exquisite structure of my frame,
Should I not see the power and wisdom
Of my Creator? Who gave it the form,
So well adapted for its purposes,
Or caused the heart to beat, driving the life-
Blood through the veins and arteries? Who made
The air, the light, the elements of sight
And sound, fitted, and so well adapted
To the organs of this human frame-work?
Who framed the economy of actual
Things—gave Seasons their great variety,
Heaven its glorious concave studded
With its shining stars, back of which, in space
Fathomless and unknown, are myriads
Of other stars and systems of the first
Magnitude? Who, but a real—living
Architect, whose many works, so beauteous
And beneficial, prove Him not only
Skillful and intelligent, but also
Good, merciful and kind. Man has within
Himself a monitor—'tis conscience! which
Forces upon him the strong conviction

Of a God, and beyond the grave. a life
Immortal, and eternal.
     Bewildered in their sophistries,
The Atheist, and Casuist may scoff
And ridicule—it matters not! reason
And conscience—the small voice within—gives
The lie to their senseless speculations.
'Tis true, our faculties are limited ;
Except from Revelation, as little
Do we know of life beyond, as the unborn
Infant in its mother's womb, knows of the
Present world. The soul confined, and fettered
In its tenement of clay, sees only
Objects external, but nothing discerns
In the great Spirit Land. In His Holy
Word, God has revealed some truths mysterious,
And most precious. But the night advances ;
Let us retire.

SCENE VII.

GREENWOOD CEMETERY.—AFTERNOON.

SPIRIT.

How like some fairy dream-land
Does this place appear, peaceful and lovely.
The birds, how joyfully they sing! how sweet
The ripples of the little streams, running
From bubbling fountains—the air, how fragrant!
Zephyrs are playing 'mong the forest trees
Which cast their shadows everywhere, making
It most delightful. But see the winding
Paths; these marble spires; these domes and
    sculptured
Statuary, towering sky-ward—mirror-
Like, reflecting back the sun-rays. Tell me,
Are these the relics of the past?

DR. WISEMAN.

'Tis indeed a peaceful place—
This great City of the Dead. The empty
Turmoil of the busy world—the jarring
Sounds of human strife, and vices hideous

To behold, come not to this sacred spot,
For 'tis enchanted ground. Here, oft I come
When vexed and wearied with the cares of life,
And 'mid these slopes and new-made graves, covered
With moss and flowers, sprinkled and kept fresh
By the mist-like spray of living fountains,
My soul is hushed to peace, and my spirit
Harmonizes with the soft, sweet music
Of the little songsters, rippling brooklets,
And sighing zephyrs. Here close communion
Doth my spirit hold, with the dear Saviour
Who did say "Lo! I am with you always;"
And then again, the presence of those loved
Ones gone before, I seem to realize,
And my wrapt soul seems vanishing from earth
Into the spirit-land. Ofttimes my heart
Turns back upon itself, and I review
My life from childhood up. My mother's smile
When first I lisped the little prayer she taught,
Her loving precepts in my boyhood days,
Upon my soul are photographed.
    How pure
And innocent is childhood, when nurtured,

And rightly guided by a mother's love,
And by a mother's prayers. These I enjoyed,
And by them have been blessed. To a good old
Age my mother lived, doing her Master's
Will, and when she died, here, in this hallowed
Spot we buried her. In this silent grave
Her ashes sleep, but her spirit is with
The just made perfect. Some one has written,
" It must be sweet in childhood, to give back
The spirit to its Maker, ere the heart
Hath grown familiar with the paths of sin,
And sown to garner up its bitter fruits."
'Tis true! but how much sweeter 'tis to die,
And give one's spirit to its Author back,
When life's great work, for which it was designed
Has been accomplished. The aged Christian,
Who for three score years and ten, has battled
For his Master, avoiding sinful paths,
And garnering up most precious fruits from plants
Transplanted—who has lived an active life
In doing good to others; giving bread
To starving thousands—to the afflicted
A sympathizing heart; Oh! such an one,

Matured in holiness, and strong in faith,
Will in his dying moments, hear the voice—
The still small voice, whispering in his ear,
" Well done, thou good and faithful servant ; " he
Will see a crown of glory—the Victor's
Crown suspended o'er his head, and Angels,
All clothed in spotless white, waiting to waft
Him to the skies. The good man dies, and falls
Asleep in Jesus. To the memory
Of the departed, these shrines and marble
Slabs, sculptured and engraved, have been by friends
Erected, while the graves from time to time,
With rare flowers are strewn, fragrant and fresh.

SPIRIT.

Do disembodied spirits visit earth,
Mingling with those who were their relatives
And friends?

DR. WISEMAN.

It may be so;
But the great secrets of the Spirit World,
Are not to mortal eye revealed. We know
All that is good for man to know—that God
Exists, and fills immensity of space ;

That spirits from cherubim to lowest
Angel, are but ministering servants,
Sent forth on special missions to perform
His will. Would it then be strange, that He, Who
Feeds the sparrows—the lilies clothes, and counts
Our silvery hairs, should now and then, permit
The dear departed ones to visit earth,
Whispering in our hearts sweet messages
Of love, and with their presence encircling
Us, as the rainbow girdles earth ? 'Tis sweet,
Here in my favorite bower to sit
Close by my mother's grave, for here, I've felt
Her presence, and her arms of love were 'twined
About me, while the maternal kiss seemed
Pressed upon my cheek, as when a babe.

SPIRIT.

Perhaps a dream ?

DR. WISEMAN.

Dreams are a mystery !
I have read of those, who, obedient
To the mysterious guidance of their
Dreams, have the walls of old ruins clambered,

Footing found along the edge of unguarded
Battlements, forded streams, yes, clambered
Dizzy heights, and then with fixed, unseeing
Eyes to their beds return unharmed. I am
No sceptic! but how the mind can thus sway
And guide the body, blindfolded, cannot
Be explained. No! I was not dreaming, but
I seemed enraptured, or entranced. It was
Mind acting on mind; spirit communing
With spirit; the disinthralled and sinless,
Sympathizing with a soul in fetters.
With mine eyes wide, staring open, gazing
Into space, Oh! how I tried but a glimpse
To catch of her ethereal form, but could
Not—that was not permitted.

SPIRIT.

Most strange, and wonderful it is! You must
Have loved your mother?

DR. WISEMAN.

Loved! I idolized—yea, almost
Worshiped her. Pure, loving, truthful, she was
A model of her sex—of womanhood

My ideal. I but returned the love
Bestowed on me. It was her strong desire
To make her boy a preacher of God's word,
And a fit instrument for doing good
Among his fellow men. For this, she prayed
And labored. From school I entered College,
And having with high honors graduated,
I studied for the ministry—was then
Ordained, and for forty years have I preached
The everlasting gospel, which I trust
Has not been all in vain. A few years more
Will end my stewardship. But come! yonder
Is a plot, which tells a fearful tale—wouldst
Visit it, and hear the tragic story?

SPIRIT

Is it of one, who,
Like a crushed, faded blossom, aside was
Cast as worthless? or of one, who, o'ercome
By some great calamity, died broken-
Hearted? Let us go at once, and let me
Hear what thou wouldst say of human
Suffering.

DR. WISEMAN.

Man's folly is proverbial! How full
Of human blunders, ignorance and crime
Is the historic page! Besmeared with blood,
It tells of mad ambition, grasping avarice,
And venal lust—of gold, the shining ore
For which men pledge their souls—of cruel war
With all its sick'ning horrors—of griping
Want, and swollen gluttony. It recounts
What tyranny has done by dungeons, racks,
And tortures; so terrible, as to freeze
The blood within our veins, and stop the heart's
Pulsations—of bloody persecutions,
Whereby with human gore the very streest
Were flooded, when old and young, like yellow
Leaves from trees did fall—victims of the hour.

    Of these I speak not; nor shall I tell
Of pestilence and famine, which stalketh
Forth at noon-day, dragging countless victims
In their train—nor of the fierce tornado,
Fearful earthquakes, or ravenous sea, which
At times, fiend-like will swallow up those
Resting on her bosom. Thou hast seen fire?

A blessing, and a comfort to our race
When kept in proper bounds and well controlled.
Warmth it gives, and sustenance—generates
The steam which propels our ocean steamships—
Which drives huge trains of freight o'er our iron
Roads with lightning speed, and in motion sets
The complicated machinery of our
Workshops.   Once let loose, like human passions,
It becomes frightful and destructive.
                    In this great " City of Churches,"
There was erected a massive building,
To the Drama dedicated.   Modern
In style and architecture, it was built
With circles, galleries, parquet, and with
An orchestra whence issued most joyous
Music, sweet and harmonious.   The stage,
On which the Actors played their parts, covered
All o'er with scenes, draped and festooned, appeared
When lighted up with brilliant gas lights, like
Pictures in fairy land.   Lovely it looked,
One evening—seems but yesterday ;—the house
Well filled with gay and thoughtless ones, with old
And young, seemed " Pleasure's Temple," for here sat

Side by side, parents and children, brother
And sister, lover and maid seemingly
Entranced, as in wonder they gazed on scenes
And actors, or listened to sweetest strains
Of music.
    Little thought
This vast assembly, that Death had stalked
With them in by the open door, ready
Stood to play his part in the great drama
Of "The Two Orphans." The play proceeded!
In the last intended act, the curtain
Had just been raised, when Death, like an arrant
Knave, stealthily and unseen breathed upon
A jet light, driving its flickering flame
Upon a drop scene, along which, creeping
In silence, it leaped boldly on festooned
Drapery, throwing out its red-forked tongues
Of fire, like hissing serpents. One moment
Only, and the red, lurid flames burst forth
In one great mass of fire, unquenchable
And resistless. Then came another wave
Of black, dense smoke, rising from pit to dome;
Shut in by high, strong walls, it filled the house

With hot, sulphureous air, and vapors
Most obnoxious. Here, there, and everywhere,
Flitting shadows could be seen of half-crazed
Men, fainting women, and frightened children,
Jostling, crowding, crushing, each the other,
As shrieking and panic-stricken, they rushed
Headlong towards the exit. Others hurried
To and fro, crying for help, but no one
Heeded. It was a race for life! each one
Must save himself, and the hot brain was racked
Till it became delirious. And still
The fire most pitiless did rage, darting
Its bright, burnished fangs into the faces
Of its victims, gasping and suffocated
From the smoke compressed. Nothing could avail!
And the great surging mass of human life,
Together went through the broken flooring,
Down into one common grave. Three hundred,
Moth-like perished.

    O Death! how merciless
Thou art! thou didst stand a cold skeleton,
Heartless, fleshless, bloodless, gazing upon
The work of thine own hand—upon this heap

Of mangled, torn, and scorched humanity.
More cruel art thou than the Emperor
Solyman, the heartless Turk, who killed his
Favorite in his sleep, lest pain he should
Inflict. Why not come, and take life gently,
As do the Egyptains, who, criminals
Destroy by asps—charming into quiet
Sleep their senses?
    Into ruins, crumbled
This great fabric man had reared, and from its
Smouldering embers, forth were borne, the charred
Remains of many victims. In this spot,
Fourscore and ten were buried! Here they rest,
In one great, common grave.

    SPIRIT.

    Thy words are heart-rending.
I do not envy man, nor his estate,
For Death like spectral shadow, seems ever
On his track.

    DR. WISEMAN.

    True, all must die!
But when, or how, we know not, for Death comes
As doth a thief, and takes us unawares.

The great curse, "*Thou shalt surely die*," man brought
Upon himself by wilful disobedience.
God perfect is! sinless and pure! and so
Was man; but when temptation came he fell,
And scattered evils, thickly as shells on
Ocean's sands. Since it must come, it matters
Little when we die, if but prepared. Dust
Unto dust returns, but the Spirit unto
God who gave it. Death loosens the silver
Cord—breaks the golden bowl—into pieces
Dashes the crystal urn. Like the pitcher
Broken at the fountain, or wheel broken
At the cistern, so our frail bodies,
Worthless are cast aside. What matters it!
The soul unfettered will go up to God
Pure as a snow-flake, and bright as evening
Star, will shine forever and forever.

In Memoriam.

In Memoriam.*

Life is most mysterious!
What makes the heart to throb—the pulse to beat,
And through the system drives the warm life-blood,
Thence to the heart returns it? What power
Invisible starts this human time-piece,
So fearfully and wonderfully made?
Whence comes the breath that makes the living-
    soul—
A soul, immortal and unchangeable?
           'Tis not by chance!
The same Almighty Power that fixed the laws,
Absolute and eternal, which govern
All shining worlds and countless stars, which has
Thickly strewn infinity with grandeur,
Created man—the noblest work of God!
           Death, too, is most mysterious!
What is death? Is it a famished Vampire,
A Spirit Fiend, heartless and invisible.

Which comes and goes at will, as blood-hounds
Go, scenting the tracks of frightened victims?
Will seize a King sitting upon his throne,
Or beggar in the street, and to the same
Cold grave consign them—crush the fair maiden
Sauntering 'mong the flowers, or can kill
The infant, innocent and beautiful,
While smiling in his very face? No, no!
This mysterious something we call Death,
Is but the hand of God—of Him, whose great
Omniscient eye gazes far down into
The dark future, and doeth all things well.
Grieve not, O mother! for thy cherub boy,
Whose cheek crimsoned with purest life-blood,
And whose head covered all o'er with clustering
Ringlets, was laid gently upon thy bosom,
As lisping his simple prayer, he quickly
Fell asleep, dreaming of white-robed Angels,
Even while Death taking the form of croup,
Noiselessly, stealthily appeared, and from
The lovely casket, took the bright jeweled
Spirit. Grieve not! for its brief work was done,
And thus unfettered, it went up to God

Pure as a snow-flake, and bright as Evening
Star, will shine forever and forever.
                Who has not lost a friend?
Or standing o'er the cold and silent grave,
Has not watered it with gushing, scalding
Tears, as memories of the past, crowded
The burdened mind? A few days since—but
    yesterday,
We performed the last sad rite the living
Owe the dead—*the burial of our Father.*
                Among the masses of mankind,
There have in every age been found, good men,
Whose characters like burnished gold, have shone
Spotless and pure. Generous, unselfish,
Full of faith and holy love, they have lived
Not for themselves, but to promote the good
Of others, and magnify the Great Name
Of Him who governs all. Like oases
In a barren desert, so in the moral
World, where everything seems scorched, and
    shriveled
Up by sin, such characters look fruitful
And most refreshing. Unknown, unhonored

They may be—on history's page their names may
Not be written—it matters not! for in
The great Book of Life, they are enrolled.
           Such was our father!
Venerable in years, rich in experience,
Strong in faith, and with a heart most loving
And sympathetic, he dwelt among us
Encircled by God's presence, as rainbow
Girdles earth.
His life went out, as day ofttimes departs
In glorious sunset, leaving all earthly
Things arrayed in glory—adorned with tints
Of purple, crimson, and of gold. Upon
Its mother's bosom, the tender infant
Nursed, petted and caressed, will smile and fall
Asleep in happy innocence; and thus
This aged man, strong in his faith, and full
Of love and holy zeal, did breathe his last,
And without suffering or pain, sweetly
Did fall asleep in Jesus.
           As forest leaves about to die,
Put on their loveliest hues, thus did he die,
With crest, and coat of arms upon his heart

And conscience stamped, while on his brow appeared
The imprint of nobility.   In light,
And glory, as the old year went to its
Grave, with all the autumnal glories
In its train, so passed he away—not bound
An unwilling captive, to the chariot
Wheel of the all conquering Death, but went
In a triumphal march, with victory
Perched upon his banner, and to his Soul's
Coronation.
Four thousand times an hour, for ninety, and three
Years, his faithful heart, night and day had throbbed,
Keeping in motion the current of his
Life blood; but his work was done, and on God's
Holy day, at early dawn, he rested
From his labors.   Rest thee, our father!
While the frail body crumbles into dust,
The soul immortal has gone up to God,
With powers well suited for the spirit world.

---

* Mr. Elisha Bliss, of Hartford, Conn., ninety-three years of age, and with one exception, the oldest male resident of that city, died on Sunday morning, January 2, 1881. There had been a gathering of his children and grand children on New Year's night, and he had seemingly enjoyed himself very much, taking an active part in the social exercises and amusements of the evening. Bidding all good night, he retired about 10 o'clock. He was found dead in his bed the next morning, lying in his usual position and with the bed-clothing undisturbed. His lamp of life had gone out, even without flickering.

Miscellaneous.

MISCELLANEOUS.

THE MISER'S FATE.

The Miser entered his vile abode,
Placed the cross-bar on the door,
Examined the locks—examined the bolts,
"All safe," as ever before.

No sunlight, or moonlight, or starlight,
Entered that darkened cell;
But he lit his two-penny candle,
Like a watchman, saying "all's well!"

Then went he to one of the corners;
A corner under his cot,
In the floor, a secret door opened,
A door he never forgot.

His treasures of gold, and of silver,
Upon the table he laid,.
All faded with age and covered with mould,
A huge, massive pile they made.

Thirsty, and supperless, down he sat,
And spread out his hoarded store,
He counted it once—he counted it twice,
Three times he counted it o'er.

'Twas a terrible night! so frosty and cold,
The wind most viciously blew,
It rocked the old hovel, rushed through the cracks,
It chilled him through, and through.

Still colder it grew! the mercury fell
Some twenty degrees below;
No fire on his hearth! no fuel! no food!
Through each crevice sifted the snow.

He laid himself down on his coverless bed,
And clasped to his chilly breast,
The God of his heart—his silver and gold,
And sank to his cheerless rest.

Did they give him warmth? those golden coins,
Did they thaw out his freezing veins?
Did they nourish, and strengthen the physical man ?
Did they soothe and lessen his pains?

This man of rags—unshaven, unshorn,
Next day was found on his bed,
With a smile on his face, a ghastly smile—
Still hugging his idols—*but dead.*

Enshrouded in gold, he lay "in state,"
There was gold behind and before,
There was gold at his head, and gold at his feet,
To be counted by him—*nevermore!*

A spectral burglar had entered the door,
'Mid the storm, and hurricane's breath,
And stole, not the gold, but the life, and the soul
Of the wretch—*that burglar was Death.*

A MIDNIGHT TRAGEDY.

Brutes know their foes by instinct, and if one
Approaches, they will fly, or brace themselves
For battle. The wren, the most diminutive
Of all the feathered tribe, seeing a bird
Of prey, will in some darkened corner, or
In some quiet nook, its young secrete, and
If there attacked—will to the last defend
Them. The mother-fowl, instinctively broods
Her little ones, and with her body makes
A breast-work for their safety, ere the hawk,
Poising himself in mid air, and swooping
Down can reach them. The feeblest worm that
    crawls
If trodden on, turns on its foe and seeks
Revenge. Can man do less? If ignobly
Wronged, he will be avenged let come what may;
And if assaulted, will himself defend,
Though he take life in doing it.

The sun had set.—The shades of night
Were densely gathering, when I, a wearied
Traveler, stopped at a village inn, in the
Far West. 'Twas in the month of August, hot
And sultry day, and not a breath of air
To fan my feverish brain, as dust covered
I alighted from my horse, and gave my
Orders—both for man and beast. It was
A quiet house; the landlord, thoughtful man,
Bestirred himself to do my bidding.
'Tis true, some idlers
Could be seen, lounging about the bar-room—
Rough-looking men, who with a smack drank down
Vile whiskey, keeping however, an eye
Upon the stranger as if bent on mischief.
I retired to rest,
And, wearied as I was, soon fell asleep;
Not soundly did I sleep, for nervousness
Had made me restless. Soon midnight came,—dead
Hour when good men are at rest, but ruffians
Are abroad; when fiends do yell, and crimes
Are perpetrated. Little did I dream
That even then, one of the lowest class,

A most inhuman wretch! assassin-like—
Armed to the teeth, was slyly creeping in
Upon me! Stealthily he came, and in.
My flesh his poisoned fangs he thrust, and with
Gluttonous appetite—cannibal-like was
Drinking up the life-blood of my being,
And I woke up in agony. Oh! how
I started up—went bounding out of bed
After my murderous foe, and having struck
A light, I pressed him hotly,—to the wall
I drove him, and obtained revenge. I killed
Him there!—*the villainous mosquito.*

WESTMINSTER.

READ AT THE FIFTH ANNIVERSARY OF WESTMINSTER CHURCH, BLOOMFIELD, N. J., HAVING BEEN ORGANIZED BY CERTAIN MEMBERS, WHO WITHDREW FOR THAT PURPOSE FROM THE FIRST PRESBYTERIAN CHURCH.

Once on a time, within my garden wall,
In a quiet nook, where light and dew did fall,
I had transplanted with the greatest care
A little tiny twig—valued, and rare;
No tender infant at its mother's breast,
With careful nursing, could have been more blest;
But yet, its fresh leaves drooped—and at my feet,
Alone, in solitude it seemed to weep.
I knew it would not die—that cherished flower—
For it was watered by an April shower;
Refreshed, revived, it raised its drooping head,
And kissed the sunbeams playing round the bed.
From this time on, as if by magic power,
It grew in strength—in beauty every hour;
With pride I pruned its branches, shaped its form,
Strengthened its roots, secured it from the storm.

Five years had passed!—the twig was then a tree,
Mere sapling it is true, but I could see
Choice fruit suspended, which a lesson taught;
Our lives should active be— with good works fraught.
Wide are its branches now, its roots are deep,
A refuge from the storm—from Summer's heat;
Rich in its fruits, with pleasure I recall
This dear old tree, beside the garden wall.

Once on a time, near by our village green,
A neat and rustic chapel could be seen,
In a quiet nook, 'mid the sunbeams fair,
Our infant church has been transplanted there.
This beauteous flower from its mother's breast
So gently had we plucked, it seemed at rest;
This Heavenly plant, with zealous care and fears,
Nourished in love, we watered with our tears;
Around our hearts, its tendrils it did twine,
In strength and beauty grew this fruitful vine;
First, blossoms came, then purple fruit it bore,
By careful pruning it produced the more.

Five years have passed! This infant church is now
A tower of strength, and on her matchless brow

Enthroned in innocence, is smiling Love,
With her attendant Graces from above.
How strong in faith! in joyous hope, how bright!
Like rising sun, she scatters beams of light;
In good works active, for the poor a care,
Fervent in Spirit—diligent in prayer,

Then onward in Faith! for you now behold
The buds and blossoms all fringed with gold;
The ripening fruit, with its foliage green,
In various colors may be seen.

Then onward in Hope! your future is bright,
The clear sun by day, the bright stars by night
Will lighten your pathway—will cheer you on
In the noble work, so well begun.

Then onward in Love! united and strong!
Build up what is right, discard what is wrong;
Onward and upward, our motto shall be,
For time, and through all Eternity.

GIVE US THIS DAY, OUR DAILY BREAD.

" Give us this day, our daily bread ; "
How often asked—how thoughtless said,
But 'tis a general term, you know,
As used by mortals here below.

" Give us our daily bread " we pray,
All use it rightly; the same way,
But 'tis a comprehensive prayer,
Implying several kinds of ware.

One means a crust a bit of meat,
An Irish stew, unfit to eat,
Some cast-off clothing—hut of clay ;
His *summum bonum*, day by day.

One means good, substantial food,
(Meat once a day is understood)
Milk for the children—space to roam,
A rustic cottage—quiet home.

One means more than a simple dish,
For after soup, he wants his fish;
Then orders on the roast beef rare,
Has just commenced his sumptuous fare,
For on the side-board soon appear
Pies, dumplings, puddings, coffee clear,
Ices and cream—and in the train
Come sparkling wines, and choice champagne.

The man of fashion—nice and prim,
Thinks of new suits, "nobby" and trim;
His wife, of course, must have her share,
She goes for silks and diamonds rare.

The millionaire, with wealth untold,
Clings to his bonds, and stocks, and gold,
And prays for more—petition strains
To take in profits, rents and gains.

The politician as of yore,
Means office, plunder, and a score
Of other things—he ne'er forgets
To call them "*honest perquisites.*"

Our prayer should be, our daily bread,
In peace, contentment to be fed ;
If we have wealth—of goods a store,
To make us Almoners to the poor.

REFLECTIONS.

ON THE DEATH OF A DEAR FRIEND.

As Autumn leaves are dropping,
Touched by an early frost,
As sweetest flowers are blasted,
And all their fragrance lost;

As evening shadows flitting,
Will from our pathway glide,
Like sunbeams which go dancing,
Like ebb and flood of tide;

As wave upon the ocean,
Dies on the sandy shore,
Like ripple on the water,
Which sinks for evermore;

As mighty ships are stranded,
Beneath the maelstrom's sway,
As midnight dreams most vivid,
Do quickly pass away;

Like bubble floating in the air,
Like rainbow, changeable, but fair,
Like pearl-drop in an infant's eye,
Like snow-flake from an April's sky;

Thus *Human Life* is fleeting,
A moment's space—no more!
To-day we live—to-morrow die,
And our brief toil is o'er.

Another light extinguished,
Another spirit fled,
Another form lies lifeless
In its cold and silent bed.

Another heart ceased throbbing,
Another pulse is still,
Another saint in glory
Doing her Maker's will.

With golden harp, with sceptre bright,
All clothed in robes of dazzling light
Her ransomed spirit now at rest,
Forever with the Angels blest.

LIFE AND DEATH.

Earth to earth, and dust to dust!
Gold will tarnish—steel will rust,
Flowers will fade, and dazzling light
Of brightest day, will change to night.

Earth to earth, and dust to dust;
Storms will gather—bubbles burst,
The sea will yawn—wild waters hiss,
While wrecks go down in the abyss.

Earth to earth, and dust to dust;
In human strength we cannot trust,
Dreams will vanish—hopes decay,
And noon-day glory fade away.

Earth to earth, and dust to dust;
Die we may, and die we must,
Joys will change to bitter sorrow—
Life to-day—but death to-morrow.

Earth to earth, and dust to dust ;
The rich, the poor, the vile, the just ;
All will be changed—for all must die,
Each in his narrow grave will lie.

Earth to earth, and dust to dust ;
What matters it ?—the Soul will burst
Its shackles !—free from earthy sod,
'Twill mount unfettered to its God.

CHRISTMAS HYMN.

RECITED ON CHRISTMAS EVE, BEFORE THE SABBATH SCHOOL OF
WESTMINSTER CHURCH, BLOOMFIELD, N. J.

Another year is past and gone,
Another festive season come,
With sparkling eyes—with joyous face
We crowd this sacred, holy place.

Westminster! Endearing name!
She claims no titles, wealth or fame,
No stately dome, no belfry high,
No turrets pointing to the sky ;

No ivory throne, no glorious nave,
No sculptured figures of the brave,
No groined roof—no tombs of Kings,
No crumbling monuments she brings ;

No images of saints in gold,
No transepts, cloisters as of old,
No high mass said—no low mass done,
No Prelate's voice, "*Dominus vobiscum.*"

Bedecked alone with fragrant flowers,
Culled by fair hands from Nature's bowers,
This young church stands, as she *will stand*,
A model from the Master's hand.

Within these gates may Peace and Love,
Bring richest blessings from above,
Our songs of praise—our solemn prayer,
Bespeak, O Lord! thy presence here.

To our loved Pastor, who has striven
To lead our wandering souls to heaven,
Our heartfelt thanks we give, and pray
That God will bless him day by day.

Our Superintendent's smiling face,
Beaming with love and heavenly grace,
With welcome hearts we ever greet,
When in the Sabbath School we meet.

Teachers! to you, our thanks we owe,
For kindness—watchful care you show,
For good works done, instruction given,
Turning our thoughts from earth to heaven.

God bless all worlds, God bless the earth,
God bless the land that gave us birth—
Our church, our school, this festive sight,
God bless us all! Good Night! Good Night!

www.ingramcontent.com/pod-product-compliance
Lightning Source LLC
Chambersburg PA
CBHW020910230426
43666CB00008B/1389